Eat This Too!

Eat This Too!

**It'll Also Make
You Feel Better**

by Dom DeLuise

POCKET BOOKS
New York • London • Toronto • Sydney • Tokyo • Singapore

POCKET BOOKS, a division of Simon & Schuster Inc.
1230 Avenue of the Americas, New York, NY 10020

Designed by Levavi & Levavi

Library of Congress Cataloging-in-Publication Number: 97-69715

ISBN: 0-671-00431-X

First Pocket Books hardcover printing December 1997

10 9 8 7 6 5 4 3 2 1

Printed in the U.S.A.

Mamma Mia

I dedicate this book to my warm and wonderful mom, Vincenza DeStefano DeLuise, who came to this country when she was twenty years old and made a life here with Papa and gave me, my brother and sister an opportunity to grow up in the U.S.A. God bless America. And God bless my mother's cooking—her bravery—her cooking—her love—and, of course, her cooking. Thank you, Mamma.

ELLIS ISLAND
1892–1992
TM © 1987 SL/EIF, INC.

The Statue of Liberty-Ellis Island Foundation, Inc.

proudly presents this

Official Certificate of Registration

in

THE AMERICAN IMMIGRANT WALL OF HONOR

to officially certify that

Vincenza-Giovanni DeLuise

came to the United States of America from

• Italy •

joining those courageous men and women who came to this country in search of personal freedom, economic opportunity and a future of hope for their families.

Lee A. Iacocca
The Statue of Liberty-Ellis Island
Foundation, Inc.

LIBERTY
1886·1986

Contents

Introduction: Soup to Nuts

*F*ood is a very friendly thing to do with your friends. If it's hot and delicious and you're in a comfortable chair and you have a glass of good wine to sip and you share old memories and good humor, the times that you pass with your friends can be quite delicious and memorable. Carol and I really enjoy having friends over to our home. We have a dining room table that seats about twelve people and our chairs are comfortable. There's three inches of foam under your bottom when you're at our table. I usually create, or Carol creates, some sort of centerpiece that has to do with our guests, the season, or the holiday. Since everybody is conscious of fat content lately, especially in California, I serve crudités with a nonfat dip and the healthiest appetizers I can: mushrooms, shrimp, or nonfat cheeses.

Serving food hot is a very important thing. I like people to see steaming soup being ladled into their bowls so I really am an advocate of soup tureens. I make sure, for example, that chicken is cooked just before you eat it so it's served from the oven to the table. Sometimes I serve chicken cooked in an oven with steamed vegetables. I have a gas burner on the table and my bamboo steamer is cooking the vegetables while we're having the salad. After the salad plates are removed the chicken is served and I uncover the steaming vegetables to "oohs" and "aahs."

Often we start with grace said by me or a guest or one of the kids. Sometimes people will say a standard grace but more often than not, they are very poetic, funny, touching. We all join hands and there's a minute of grace talk that can remind us all of how lucky we are, but it's never long enough to make the food cold!

Dessert is often nonfat yogurt with my no-sugar apple pie and if there's a current fruit in season like strawberries or watermelon or cantaloupe, we use those as well. If we have a larger gathering people will bring their favorite desserts and I put them on the buffet table and everyone nibbles to their heart's content!

My favorite time is when people are having coffee or tea sitting on comfortable chairs, talking, listening, and laughing. The highlight of the evening for me is the sharing that goes on after the meal. When you leave our table you're nourished by the food, but more often than that, your heart and soul are nourished by the conversation, the sharing, and the laughter and love. Carol and I are really blessed with incredible friends. Viva Amigos!

Fathers and Sons

When I was young, my father was a very demonstrative parent. He shouted and raged quite a lot, so as I grew up I became a person with a child within me that was kind of damaged. My father scared me with his yelling and his confrontational nature.

So when Carol and I got married and we had three sons, I made a silent vow to myself that I was going to be a very understanding father and that I was going to be a companion, a friend to my children. However, from time to time, I would hear myself shouting the same things my father said to me that I vowed I would never say.

I made a conscious effort not to be scary like my father, but instead to be nurturing like my mother. That may, in fact, have messed me up pretty good, because I have kept a lot of shrinks pretty busy with figuring out just who I am. Now that I am older, and after a lot of mind searching, I've come to the conclusion that I'm okay. I'm at peace with myself and generally have good intentions. Oh, yes, occasionally I do get in touch with my "shadow" side and some of my anger, but thanks to Jung, that's okay, too.

There are times when you say something to a child, and they hear it in the purest sense of the word, and it gets stored in their "computer," and it really ain't what you meant. It sometimes turns out humorously!

There was one day when my oldest son, Peter, was a little boy. We were in a supermarket and I showed him an orange with the word "Sunkist" stamped on it, and said, "That's how you can tell when they're ready!" I'm sure that my joke confused him, because about one month later he came to me with a half-eaten orange from our backyard tree and said, "Look, Dad, God forgot to write 'Sunkist' on this orange." I have always wondered if Peter and oranges have ever been the same since!

My Three Sons

Peter

Peter, our oldest boy, got out of high school and was in a TV series called "21 Jump Street" for five years. It was pretty clear that all of our sons wanted to be actors and—God bless them—they are doing pretty well.

Peter has been in a lot of TV and films, and he and Michael worked together in Florida with Roy Scheider on a science-fiction show called "Sea Quest." Michael had gills and Peter played an android that had gone bad. He had the strength of a bull and the disposition of a four-year-old. Peter is a highly accomplished actor, very gifted, so that when he performed that role he often could and did break your heart.

He is also an accomplished director and a very talented writer. He just completed a screenplay entitled *Between the Sheets,* directed by his brother Michael, and starring him in the leading role. Nepotism aside, David, their younger brother, Carol, their mother, and me, their father, got jobs in the film, and I for one say "Go for it! All right!"

Peter and I just completed a script that we wrote together. I did some of the talking and he did most of the writing. I found that he was a gentle partner, very attentive to what I said, and very accomplished when it came to getting the ideas down on paper. He was faster than fast and I'm looking forward to performing in our film, "Cacciatore Ghost." Thank you, Peter.

When the DeLuises get together and we have a heated family discussion, it is Peter who is the negotiator. We call him "Switzerland" because he manages to stay so neutral.

I'm glad to call my oldest boy Peter "my friend."

Michael

Our son Michael, the middle boy, is different from Peter and David, who are both big boys with hearty appetites, in many ways. When Michael was a little boy he would ask for half a glass of milk and half a cookie. I knew he was my son but I wondered where his genes came from.

He began his career with lots of television and over a ten-week period on "21 Jump Street." Michael does very well and is a director and writer as well as an actor. He just produced *Between the Sheets* written by and starring Peter. When he was on "Sea Quest" he looked like he had taken a Jimmy Cagney pill. He developed a great character, who in the sci-fi show "Sea Quest" had gills and could breathe underwater. After two years on that show Michael increased his breathing capacity tenfold.

He was recently on "NYPD Blue" playing Dennis Franz's son and did a really phenomenal job, and if you don't believe me you can ask his mother. At the present moment he is beginning a new TV series called "Brooklyn South" created by Steven Bochco, who is also responsible for "NYPD Blue."

Michael plays the piano. He can also walk on his hands and do a back flip landing on his feet. He can also lasso your heart and make you feel embraced from a good ten feet away.

David

When David was born I used to call him "My gift from God." Being the youngest, he was the easiest to raise. He is full of fun, vivacious and very much a risk-taker. He and his lovely wife Brigitte have a great and beautiful child, Riley, who is the grandchild of grandchildren. I really think she is a genius but ask *any* grandfather. He'll tell you.

David is a consummate actor and when he was eight years old he starred as my son in a TV movie I produced called "Happy." He is a very natural actor as I found out when David was very young. He would come to me complaining about Peter and Michael teasing him, and all the time sobbing. I would reprimand Peter and Michael for anything David said they did. Since he was crying I believed him. Then one day I said, "Let's play an acting game," and I told David to pretend his dog had died. He immediately burst into copious amounts of realistic tears. I had a realization and I asked David, "When you come in complaining about Peter and Michael, are they real tears or are they these kind of tears that you are using now?" David smiled broadly, followed by a sheepish grin. From that moment on I stopped reprimanding Peter and Michael. We all laugh about it now.

David is now a parent and a very good one at that, I must say. Riley DeStefano (my mother's maiden name) DeLuise keeps Brigitte (who is really a great mother) and David on their toes. They are a very happy family, who are all expecting another baby. My second grandchild! WOWEE!

Nina Hirschfeld's Dad

*T*he *New York Times* has a theatrical section on Sunday that has the power to enrich your week if you can get hold of it wherever you are. There's a brilliant cartoonist who has been drawing for them for a very long time, Al Hirschfeld. He takes the essence of someone's features and usually does a picture that can make you famous, if you ain't already. Years ago I had my picture done by him and was able to sit with him and his lovely wife in their brownstone and have lunch. Can you imagine? He looks very wise because of his white beard and he met me and did a picture of me without my beard and then years later did a picture of me with my beard. It was an enormous form of flattery! He is just fantastic. There was recently a documentary on Hirschfeld called "The Line King" and Carol and I saw it at the Academy. His life has been awesome and his spontaneous humor gets giant laughs. He is a very witty man!

When I did *Die Fledermaus* at the Metropolitan Opera in New York, Carol very thoughtfully and graciously got him to do a picture of me as the character of Frosch. I was very flattered when Carol presented the picture to me backstage. She told people that I was going to be very surprised but I was more flattered since Hirschfeld is one of my favorite artists in the world. Twenty years ago when I was having lunch with him, I asked him where he worked and he took me to his studio upstairs. It was on the top floor of his brownstone and it was a room that he had worked in since the early forties. There were pictures on the wall that he had pinned up literally more than fifty years ago—Claudette Colbert, Greta Garbo, Robert Benchley, a depiction of the Algonquin Round Table with all those famous writers. The man is awesome and his skill dazzles both Carol and me.

HIRSCHFELD

I was in his room and I said, "Is this where you do it?" He said, "Right here." There was a stool that faced a very large piece of wood like a drafting table that was tilted down so he could work on it easily. He puts a piece of paper down and holds each corner down with a pin. Since he must have been at this table for sixty years there were four giant holes made up of the cluster of all the pinpricks. I said to him, "What does it feel like to be the greatest cartoonist in the world?" He was very gracious. He said, "Every time I look at the blank piece of paper, I think, 'I hope I can still do this!'" I was surprised that his vast talent was accompanied by any doubt at all. I was also thrilled because I have found that when I meet great achievers, they are also in touch with the frightened child inside them.

He has a lovely daughter named Nina and there are so many people who love to find the Ninas in his pictures. When he first did me there was one Nina in the small wisps of hair at the top of my head. Chita Rivera has the caricature in the folds of her dress. Can you imagine being famous because your father is a cartoonist and has your name magically appear in the beard, eye, or bow tie of some famous person's picture? After Carol presented me with the picture of Frosch, we had some tea at his home. By now he was ninety and amazingly alert. His wife had passed away and he had remarried. He was very gracious as he looked at my children's book and he complimented Christopher Santoro who did the illustrations. I thought that was great! As we sat having tea, the phone rang and he said, "Money!" as he got up to answer it. We chatted a long time and he let us take some pictures, which was very kind of him. Then the phone rang again and much to our amusement, he said, "More money!" and answered the phone.

I know that his work has brought me great pleasure but it is also very clear that Hirschfeld has brought great pleasure to the world. I recently presented my wife Carol with his impression of her. I think it is fantastic. Carol was speechless and thrilled. Notice her necklace—it has nineteen Ninas. People are thrilled if they only have one. Carol said if I never gave her another thing as long as she lives she'll be happy with her Hirschfeld.

Thank you, Mr. Hirschfeld!

Oh, Sister, Please Don't Bite It: My Childhood in Brooklyn, U.S.A.

During the hot summer vacation, all the kids in Brooklyn used to go to Coney Island to swim in the ocean. We'd take the subway and it only cost a nickel. If you needed money, you could pick up empty soda bottles and take them to "the man" and get two cents for each bottle. So when we were at Coney Island, if we needed money, we would collect empty bottles.

Honestly, though, a penny in those days was worth something. For instance, my mother used to give me five cents and I would go to Sam's on the corner, and with that five cents I'd end up with a small Hershey bar for three cents, a penny for a pretzel and the last penny for a pickle that you'd have to reach into a barrel filled with vinegar for. I guess this was my first official snack.

On the way home, I'd eat the chocolate, the pretzel, and the pickle. Since they were all different sizes, you had to bite each of them strategically so you could finish them all at the same time. When I think about it, I cannot imagine what my breath must have smelled like.

For ten cents, during the summer months, you could get a Charlotte Russe, a small piece of cake in a round paper cylinder that was filled with whipped cream with a cherry on top. It looked like an ice-cream cone, and was another memorable snack.

Then there was the Mellow Roll. It was also ten cents, but, oh, it was worth it. It was a cylinder of ice cream wrapped on the outside with paper. The ice-cream man would unwrap it and stick it in a special Mellow Roll cone. My sister and I would each get one. My sister, Anne, was a "biter," and I was a "licker." She would bite her Mellow Roll and finish it, while I gently licked mine.

However, when Anne would finish hers, she became very dangerous. "Can I have some of yours?" she would ask innocently. "Are you going to lick it, or are you going to bite it?" I'd ask. I never understood how she could consume that much ice cream that quickly. "I'm going to lick it," she said. "I don't believe you, Anne," I said. "Do you really promise to lick it?" And she said, "I promise I'll just lick it." And me, like a fool, trusted her. Every time.

So I gave her my ice cream and, of course, she bit it. She never licked it. Never.

Years went by before I finally realized that "No, you can't have any of my ice cream," was an all-right answer. After all, my sister, Anne, was a known biter. If I tell this story today in her presence, she laughs and covers her face with both hands, she is so ashamed. And she should be ashamed because when someone bites your ice cream over and over and over again, and you think they're going to lick it, you end up spending a lot of time on a couch with a shrink.

Though I have moved away and live in Los Angeles and my sister lives on Long Island I have it on very good authority that she still bites ice cream.

The other day, my wife, Carol, and I went out for nonfat yogurt. She had vanilla and chocolate, and I had strawberry. She finished hers much too quickly as far as I'm concerned and asked if she could taste mine. "What?" I said quickly. "No way. Are you going to bite it or lick it? You're probably going to bite it. No. No."

I realize that my wife of thirty years can probably be trusted with my nonfat yogurt, but oh the scar runs deep when your older sister, Anne, who you love and trust, bites instead of licks.

11-Cent Movies in Brooklyn

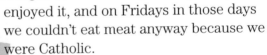

My mother, Vincenza, was a very sweet lady. Everybody on the block called her Jenny. When I was growing up she always said, "Eat this and it will make you feel better," which is the name of my first cookbook.

When you're growing up and you're poor, you don't really have any way of knowing that. I think I was the last to know. Every Friday, for instance, we had stew. It had every kind of vegetable you could imagine in a tomato sauce with no meat. I thought the stew was perfectly fine, I enjoyed it, and on Fridays in those days we couldn't eat meat anyway because we were Catholic.

When I grew up and I went to my friend Salvatore Orena's house to eat, his mother made stew with meat in it. "Whoa! You put meat in your stew?" said I. "What a great idea. Why wasn't I told?" I guess what you don't have, you don't miss.

If I went to the movies, my mother gave me one dime and one penny. Going to the movies when I was a little kid cost eleven cents. My mother didn't give up the eleven cents easily; you had to negotiate. Sometimes on Saturday, she'd give me the eleven cents and I'd see two movies, a cartoon, coming attractions, and the news. Wonderful. Then on Sunday, I'd ask, "Can I go to the movies again today?" My mother always said, "No, Papa doesn't want you to." And, of course, I would go right to my father and ask him if it was all right to go to the movies today.

Now, my father was an Italian immigrant and had a heavy accent, couldn't read or write, and was completely uninvolved in any of these shenanigans. "I non care, Dom, for me is okay if you go to the movie." "Gee, thanks, Pa."

So, I'd go back to my mother and tell her I asked Papa and he said it was okay for me to go, and then my mother would say, "Papa told me no yesterday." She usually got away with that answer, but sometimes she would break down and actually give me eleven cents two days in a row.

I recently went to the movies with my wife and the tickets were $8.50 each. How far we've come from me having to talk my mother out of eleven cents.

Two Cents Plain

Nowadays if you have change in your pocket, it's annoying. Anything under a dollar seems useless. However, when I was a kid, for two cents you could get a big glass of seltzer. For three more cents they would put in chocolate syrup, and for two more cents a little milk, and you'd have an egg cream, a New York soda drink. It cost seven cents and it was absolutely delicious. I know that when it rained I would sit by the window and pretend to fish. Our family lived on the first floor so I never caught anything but weeds from the garden. There used to be a lot of guys selling specific things like watermelon and they would shout "Watermeloooon." Sometimes fish, not a large selection, but fish nevertheless. There was a guy who had a metal chest of drawers. In the bottom drawer there was a fire and in each higher drawer, potatoes. He would shout, "Mickeys, get your hot Mickeys." For one penny you could get a baked potato wrapped in newspaper that was delicious on cold days. For two cents you could have a sweet potato, which was even better. If it was your birthday, you were definitely in for a sweet potato.

Me and Salt, Garlic and Olive Oil

*T*o be or not to be? That is the sodium! Whether to use salt to get the snow in the driveway to melt or to use salt to see whether your blood pressure goes up or not. In some tribes in Africa they use salt as we do money—this tribe has no reported cases of high blood pressure. I have not indicated the use of salt in any of the recipes.

I feel I should warn you that some of the recipes in this book do contain garlic, sometimes a hint, sometimes a lot. I wanted us to have this understanding before any further intimacies. Okay?

Olive oil helps break up cholesterol. So flavor is not the only reason we use it; it's also good for us. Besides, I'm so Italian, instead of blood, I feel I have virgin olive oil running in my veins...just for flavor!

You will find that your taste buds will be satisfied when some of the food combinations in this book get to your mouth, hit your palate, and give it those taste treats we all dream of in those kitchens of our minds! And it's so much healthier...you know! So enjoy!

Appetizers

A word on appetizers:

Appetizers = "small portions of food or drink served before the first course of a meal, such as Italian antipasto, Russian caviar, French hors d'oeuvres and the Scandinavian smorgasbord."

Picking up the custom from our European forebears, we Americans have several refinements of our own.

Start your next party or dinner with an interesting and tasty appetizer, and your guests will never miss the martinis. (Mine don't!)

TUNA FINGER SALAD

My mamma did this a lot.

1	*7-oz. can solid white tuna, drained*
3	*tablespoons nonfat mayonnaise*
2	*stalks celery, finely chopped*
1	*small onion, finely minced*
8–10	*leaves (depending on size) romaine lettuce*
1	*tablespoon capers (optional)*

Put all the ingredients except lettuce in a bowl and mix well. Place a little of the tuna mixture along the center of each romaine leaf. Arrange on a plate and you're ready to serve. Eat with your fingers!

OPTIONAL: Sprinkle lightly with grated Parmesan cheese.

SERVES 4.

STUFFED MUSHROOMS

My son David's favorite!

1   *cup seasoned bread crumbs*
1   *egg*
    chicken stock if needed
1   *tablespoon basil*
2   *tablespoons chopped onion*
    pepper to taste
    olive-oil spray
1   *pound mushroom caps (without stems)*
6   *tablespoons chicken broth*
    grated nonfat cheese

Mix bread crumbs, egg, chicken stock, basil, onion and pepper together in a bowl to make the stuffing. The mixture should be moist, but not wet.

Spray a baking dish with olive-oil spray. Fill each mushroom cavity with stuffing mixture and place in baking dish. Add 6 tablespoons chicken broth to the bottom of the baking dish. Spray stuffed mushrooms with olive-oil spray. Top with grated cheese. Bake at 350 degrees for 20–25 minutes.

SERVES 4–6.

Note: For meat stuffing, use 1 cup sautéed, drained ground turkey, beef, veal or pork.

Add to bowl with other ingredients and mix. You may need more mushroom caps. Since they vary in size, you must adjust!

The mushroom stems can be used in soups, stews, in a frittata or you can chop them up and add to bowl with other ingredients. The more volume the stuffing has, the more mushroom caps you'll need.

Great for buffets and the next day!

DEVILED EGGS

Any buffet and they are gone!

12 eggs
1/2 cup nonfat mayonnaise
4   shakes Tabasco sauce
1/2 teaspoon curry powder
1   teaspoon soy sauce
12 green olives with pimento center, cut in half (for garnish)
*   paprika*

In boiling water, hard boil the eggs, rinse in cold water, then peel. Cut eggs in half lengthwise. Remove yolks and place in a bowl or food processor. Add mayonnaise, Tabasco, curry and soy sauce to the egg yolks and mix well. (No lumps, please!) Scoop about 1 teaspoon of this mixture into the hollow egg-white center. Garnish with half of a green olive. Sprinkle eggs with a dash of paprika.

They will go like hotcakes. Oh, remember the napkins!

SERVES 6.

CRAB CAKES

Crab cakes are always a special treat. After eating mine, you'll never want the heavy fried kind again. With a little salad and some crackers, they make a very satisfying meal.

2   *pounds fresh crabmeat or imitation crab*
1   *tablespoon olive oil or cooking spray*
1   *tablespoon grated Parmesan cheese*
1   *tablespoon minced chives*
2   *eggs, beaten*
1   *teaspoon thyme*
1   *tablespoon Italian seasoning*
1   *teaspoon baking powder*
2   *tablespoons parsley*
1   *teaspoon Worcestershire sauce*
1   *cup seasoned bread crumbs*

Spray olive oil over a baking sheet.

In a large bowl, combine all the ingredients. Form the mixture into small cakes and place them on the baking sheet. Spray the crab cakes lightly with olive oil. Bake the crab cakes at 350 degrees for about 25 minutes, or until golden brown.

Serve with lemon wedges.

SERVES 4–6.

STEAMED CELERY ROOT

This is very subtle and delicious!

1   *celery root, about 1¹/₂ pounds*
2   *cups chicken broth*
1   *teaspoon lemon juice*
¹/₄ *teaspoon pepper*
2   *tablespoons butter (or 3 tablespoons fat-free Ranch dressing)*

Peel the celery root and cut into bite-size pieces. Put celery root in a medium pot and add broth, lemon juice and pepper and cook for approximately 3 to 5 minutes, or just until tender. Remove celery root from broth, add butter or Ranch dressing and serve with toothpicks.

SERVES 6.

BAKED CLAMS OREGANO

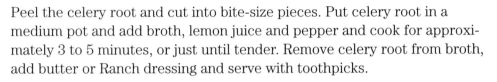

4   *garlic cloves, minced*
2   *tablespoons chopped parsley*
1   *teaspoon oregano*
¹/₂ *cup seasoned bread crumbs*
8   *tablespoons olive oil*
    pepper to taste
24 *cherrystone clams, scrubbed, opened and left on the half shell*

Add the garlic, parsley, oregano and oil to the bread crumbs, then add pepper. Blend until very smooth. Spread 1 tablespoon of the mixture over each clam on its half shell. Bake the clams uncovered at 400 degrees for about 10 minutes, or until the edges of the clams begin to curl. Do not overbake.

SERVES 4–6.

DOM'S BAKED SHRIMP BALLS

2 *pounds shelled, deveined shrimp, minced*
6 *canned water chestnuts, finely chopped*
2 *tablespoons ginger, finely chopped*
1 *onion, chopped*
2 *egg whites*
1 *teaspoon cornstarch*
3 *teaspoons olive oil*
 pepper to taste
 lemon wedges

Place everything but the lemon wedges into a bowl and mix together. Shape mixture into small balls (about 1 teaspoon). Place on a lightly greased cookie sheet. Spray balls with olive oil and bake at 350 degrees for 20 minutes. Serve hot with lemon wedges. They warm up well.

MAKES ABOUT 50 TO 60 DEPENDING ON HOW LARGE YOU MAKE THE BALLS!

ARTICHOKE APPETIZERS

My sister, Anne, loves to serve these at B-B-Qs. Me too!

1 *onion, minced*
4 *eggs, well beaten*
1/4 *cup fine dry bread crumbs*
1/8 *teaspoon pepper*
1/8 *teaspoon dried oregano*
1 *13-oz. can artichoke hearts, drained and cut into pieces*
1 *cup nonfat Cheddar cheese, grated*
1/2 *cup pimento*

Me, my sister, Anne, and my great brother-in-law, Phil.

Combine onion, eggs, bread crumbs, pepper, oregano, artichokes and cheese in a mixing bowl. Mix thoroughly. Pour evenly into a greased 11-by-7 1/2-inch baking pan. Bake at 350 degrees for 20 to 25 minutes. Allow to cool.

Cut into 1 1/2-inch squares. Serve hot, garnished with tiny pimento strips on top.

SERVES 6–8.

DOM'S MARINATED MUSHROOMS

These delicious mushrooms are first cooked. I find these mushrooms appetizing and quite different from most marinated mushrooms.

Prepare one day ahead.

2   *tablespoons olive oil*
1/2 onion, minced
2   *garlic cloves, minced*
1   *tablespoon tomato sauce*
1/4 cup dry white wine
2   *tablespoons capers*
1/8 teaspoon saffron
    freshly ground pepper to taste
1   *pound small mushrooms, brushed clean*
    juice of one lemon

Heat the oil in a small, deep casserole. Add the onion and garlic and sauté for 1 minute. Stir in tomato sauce, wine, capers, saffron and pepper. Simmer 3 minutes. Add the mushrooms to the cooking liquid, stir and simmer 1 minute more. Turn off the heat, cover, and let sit until cool. Squeeze the juice of a lemon on mushrooms. Stir. Refrigerate overnight. Serve cold or at room temperature.

These mushrooms are keepers. They're even better the next day!

SERVES 6–10.

STUFFED VINE LEAVES

1   medium onion, finely chopped
2   tablespoons olive oil
¹/₂ cup rice
¹/₂ cup pine nuts
1   tablespoon chopped fresh
    parsley
    pinch of allspice
    pinch of cinnamon
    pepper to taste
1   tablespoon tomato paste
40 (approximately) fresh grape or
    cabbage leaves, parboiled for
    1 minute
5   tablespoons strained fresh
    lemon juice

In a skillet, fry the onion in olive oil until transparent. Add the rice and fry both for a few minutes, stirring well, then add just enough water to cover the rice. Add the pine nuts, parsley and a pinch each of allspice, cinnamon and pepper. Cover and cook the mixture until the rice is dry—about 10 minutes. Stir in the tomato paste.

Using about 20 of the leaves, put a tablespoon of the stuffing in the center of each leaf. Roll up each leaf into a little parcel and place it, seam side down, in a casserole dish. Pack the rolled leaves. When all of the parcels are wedged into the dish, press an inverted saucer on top and cover them with water and the lemon juice to the level of the saucer. Set the lid on the dish and place in a 300-degree oven and bake for 25 minutes. Drain the parcels and arrange them on a platter. Serve lukewarm or chilled.

SERVES 4.

The Bad Witch of the North, Margaret Hamilton's Tuna Melt

Here I was 18 years old and working with the great Shari Lewis and Lamb Chop. I was thrilled out of my mind because I was not only working with Shari but I also had a scene disguised as a baby in the carriage with the Wicked Witch of the North from *The Wizard of Oz*, Margaret Hamilton. As mean and as green as she was in the movie, she is as gentle and sweet as she was in real life. Miss Hamilton and I talked about Mae West and W. C. Fields and I was in heaven. She said she was supposed to work only two months on *The Wizard of Oz* and ended up working two and a half years. The actress said, "I was so delighted to have all that consistent work." I thought that was funny.

She invited me to visit her at her apartment, which was in an old building, one of many surrounding a park on 14th Street. The building was built in 1900 so the elevator ride to her fourth floor apartment was unique and charming. The elevator had velvet seats, lots of carved wood with beveled mirrors, and four holes, two at the top of the elevator and two at the bottom to hold two giant ropes attached to pulleys. The elegant, gloved elevator man grabbed high on the inside rope, pulled with all his might and kept pulling hand-over-hand as we, the Wicked Witch of the North and the amazed son of a garbageman from Brooklyn, held our breath as the elegant room arrived gently on the fourth floor.

Miss Hamilton showed me many souvenirs representing highlights of her life in the theater and movies. I was thrilled, even more so as she served me a tuna melt on dark bread—something my Italian mother from Brooklyn would have looked askance at.

As the 18-year-old me ate this exotic sandwich, sipping tea from a teapot covered with a cloth tea cozy, I thought to myself, "If my friends could see me now," or as Tennessee Williams said so brilliantly in *A Streetcar Named Desire,* "Sometimes there's God so quickly."

4   *slices black Russian rye bread*

1   *7-oz. can solid white tuna, drained*

3–4 *tablespoons mayonnaise (nonfat if you like)*

8–12 *capers with a little juice*
       mustard
       pepper to taste
       Jarlsberg (or any cheese that makes you happy)

Toast the bread as you put these ingredients in a bowl. Mix well. Apply mustard to one side of the bread. Spread the tuna generously on the mustard side of the bread and place on a cookie sheet. Place on tuna an equivalent size of cheese. Broil just until cheese melts. Cut the bread in half for sandwiches or into 1½-inch squares for appetizers.

    As a sandwich this is very good with a salad and crudités—and pickles.

SERVES THE SCARECROW, THE TIN MAN AND THE COWARDLY LION. Dorothy will bring her own lunch! If you're making a sandwich it's good for one wizard.

Salads

DOM'S TOMATOES AND MOZZARELLA WITH BASIL

I like this for breakfast. By me, a staple. Fabulous appetizer with fresh hot bread.

4	*beefsteak tomatoes*
8	*ounces mozzarella, sliced*
20–30	*fresh basil leaves*
	freshly ground pepper
4	*tablespoons olive oil*

Slice tomatoes and place on a flat serving dish. Slice mozzarella. Arrange on a plate, alternating cheese and tomato. Add fresh basil leaves and pepper. Spoon oil over each helping just prior to serving.

Great with hot bread!

SERVES 4.

CHICKEN WALDORF SALAD

All this and chicken too?

3 *cups cold cooked chicken, cubed*
2 *medium apples, peeled, cored, diced and sprinkled with lemon*
    juice (to prevent browning)
2 *stalks celery, sliced*
4 *tablespoons raisins*
1 *cup coarsely chopped pecans or walnuts*
1 *tablespoon honey*
3 *tablespoons mayonnaise (nonfat, if you like)*
    white pepper to taste

    lettuce cups, avocado halves or hollowed-out tomatoes

Mix all the ingredients well. Cover and chill in the refrigerator for 2 to 3 hours.
    Serve in lettuce cups, avocado halves, or hollowed-out tomatoes. Hot bread and you have nothing to be ashamed of!

SERVES 4–6.

COLD BROCCOLI SALAD

2 *bunches broccoli, cut into florets*
4 *tablespoons olive oil*
2 *garlic cloves, minced*
   pepper to taste
   juice of one lemon

Parboil the broccoli until tender, about 3 minutes. Drain. In a large saucepan, sauté the garlic in olive oil until golden brown. Add the drained broccoli to the pan, along with pepper and lemon juice. Mix gently. Place into a serving bowl and serve warm (great) or chill for an hour and serve cold.

Serve with lemon wedges. It's even better tomorrow, if there's any left!

SERVES 4–6.

Wow, That's My Sister

My mother had three children, Nick, Anne and me. My brother is twelve years older and my sister is eight years older. My sister is a very special lady but she and I used to have little run-ins when we were growing up. I wasn't particularly good in school and my sister was a giant help to me with my homework, especially in arithmetic and spelling. To this day if I'm on the phone with her and I'm writing something, she'll help me spell a word long distance from Long Island. You know when you're a kid you think your sister is your friend? I always forced my company on my sister and her friends and she was very nice about that. She was the first to take me to Radio City Music Hall in New York and to see my first play, *Then There Were None,* a scary suspenseful play. All my life she has been my number one supporter. If I was playing Peter Rabbit

in school with a big cotton ball on my butt, or Thomas Jefferson with the same cotton spread over my head with a big black bow tie, or in a movie with Burt Reynolds and Dolly Parton, she was always cheering me on. She always applauded my entrance no matter what play I was in. My Peter Rabbit got entrance applause, my Ebenezer Scrooge got entrance applause and when I did my first off Broadway play, *The Detective Story*, with my friend Eve Roberts I received the same applause from her. I was playing detective number 2 in that play and I had about ten lines. There were eighteen people in the audience. I made my first entrance in the middle of the play and my sister, Anne, gave me tumultuous applause. The whole cast and the other seventeen people in the audience all looked at her until she finally deigned to stop clapping for her brother. If you ask me if I enjoyed it, getting applause from one person in the middle of a play, and nobody else knowing who I was, I have to say it was thrilling and even today it makes my heart smile to think that she approved of me so unconditionally. She's a great source of joy for me today and my sister and I still run "things" by each other all the time. Anne and Phil have been married almost fifty years and have three children, Concetta, John and Mary. They also have five grandchildren and really feel that they are blessed with their in-laws, Peter, Susan and Kim. She's my number one fan and I am hers. I only have one sister but if I had a chance to pick any sister anywhere in the world, I would pick Anne. When I was seven years old, though, I didn't think she was so hot. When we went to the local theater on Wednesday nights, they would give you a free dish, you'd see two movies, and sometimes they would even have a door prize. One time my sister won eight dollars. She went on stage and all the guys whistled, cheered and clapped. "Vavavoom," they said. I was in shock. I couldn't believe that my ordinary, pain-in-the-butt sister who was trying to teach me to spell was getting whistles and catcalls from the audience. "Wow, how 'bout that?" I thought. "That's my sister." And she still is. How about that? Some people have all the luck.

MY FAVORITE SISTER ANNE'S COLD CAULIFLOWER SALAD

My sis, third from left.

1   head cauliflower
4   tablespoons olive oil
4   tablespoons balsam-
    ic vinegar or lemon
    juice
2   tablespoons fresh
    basil
1/2 teaspoon oregano
2   tablespoons capers
    pepper to taste

Grab your apron. Cut cauliflower up into bite-size pieces. Place cauliflower in a pot with two cups water. Steam about 3 to 4 minutes, or until a
knife goes in easily. Drain. In a salad bowl, mix all the other ingredients
with the cauliflower. Toss gently and chill.

Serve with pride.

By the way, Anne is my *only* sister.

SERVES 2–4.

DOM'S CHINESE ASPARAGUS AND STRING BEAN SALAD

This is great warm or cold—with or without a friend.

20 *or so string beans, trimmed and cut into 2-inch pieces*
20 *or so asparagus spears (about 1 pound), trimmed and cut
     into 2-inch pieces*
1   *tablespoon freshly squeezed lemon juice*
1   *garlic clove, minced*
2   *large beefsteak tomatoes, cut into wedges
     pepper to taste*
1   *tablespoon olive oil*
1/4 *teaspoon sesame oil*
1   *teaspoon sugar*
2   *teaspoons soy sauce*
4   *lemon wedges*
4   *basil leaves*

In a steamer, bring water to a boil. Steam the string beans over medium heat for 3 minutes, then add asparagus and continue cooking both for 2 1/2 minutes longer until both are just tender. Remove from the heat and allow to cool. Combine all the remaining ingredients in a large bowl, toss gently, and serve over a bed of lettuce. Garnish with lemon wedges and fresh basil.

This also works with broccoli and/or cauliflower.

SERVES 4.

DOM'S LENTIL AND PASTA SALAD

Great on a buffet table!

4   *tablespoons olive oil*
1   *onion, minced*
2   *celery stalks, chopped*
6–8 *mushrooms, sliced*
1/2 *red pepper, diced*
1/2 *green pepper, diced*
1   *carrot, chopped*
1/2 *cup peas*
1/2 *cup corn*
1/2 *cup parsley*
2   *cups cooked, drained lentils, al dente*
2   *cups ditale (small pasta), cooked al dente*
     (or 2 cups cooked brown rice)
     pepper to taste
1/2 *tablespoon turmeric*
1/2 *cup lemon juice*
1   *cup nonfat mayonnaise*

In a large Teflon pan sauté in the olive oil the onion, celery, mushrooms, red pepper, green pepper and carrots for only about 2 minutes. Then put them along with the peas, corn, parsley, pepper, lentils and pasta in a large mixing bowl. Add pepper, turmeric, lemon juice and nonfat mayonnaise. Mix gently but thoroughly and refrigerate.

Good-good-good with anything!

Serves 10–20–?

CHICKEN SALAD

This and Madonna—you could have a great time!

2	chicken breasts cooked in white wine for 5 minutes and then cubed
1/2	cup frozen peas, cooked
1/8	teaspoon celery seed
1	carrot, shredded
2	tablespoons raisins
2	cups shredded lettuce
1	small apple, peeled and sliced (Toss with teaspoon of lemon juice to prevent browning.)
2 or 3	scallions, chopped
6	mushrooms, quartered
1	onion, sliced in crescents
2	celery stalks, chopped
1	small can water chestnuts, drained and sliced

DRESSING:

1	cup nonfat sour cream
1	tablespoon nonfat mayonnaise
3	tablespoons fresh ginger, finely minced
3	tablespoons freshly squeezed lemon juice
	freshly ground black pepper
1	tablespoon Dijon mustard

4	red cabbage or iceberg lettuce leaves
8	cherry tomatoes
1/2	cup sliced toasted almonds

Combine chicken, peas, celery seed, carrot, raisins, shredded lettuce, apple, scallions, mushrooms, onion, chopped celery and water chestnuts in a large salad bowl.

Whisk the dressing ingredients in a small bowl. Pour dressing over salad and toss. Cover and refrigerate for 1 hour.

On each salad plate, place a cabbage leaf, curved side down. Scoop salad into the leaves and garnish with cherry tomatoes and sprinkle with almond slices.

SERVES 4.

MANDARIN CHICKEN SALAD

You don't have to dress to enjoy this. This delightful combination of chicken, oranges and celery marinated in a sweet curry cream is a refreshing dish for those hot summer nights.

2   *skinless, boneless chicken breast halves (Poach in white wine just until the pink is gone.)*
      pepper to taste
1   *can mandarin oranges, drained*
1   *cup white seedless grapes, cut in half (optional)*
2   *stalks celery, chopped*
1/3 *cup plain nonfat yogurt*
1/4 *cup nonfat mayonnaise*
4   *teaspoons sugar or Sweet 'n Low*
1 1/2 *teaspoons curry powder*
1/8 *teaspoon pepper*
      parsley

Cut cold chicken breasts into bite-size pieces and place in large salad bowl.

Combine oranges, grapes, celery, yogurt, mayonnaise, sugar, curry powder and pepper in a small bowl.

Mix together with chicken. Cover bowl and chill.

Serve on lettuce leaves. Garnish with parsley.

SERVES 4.

CREAMY GARLIC PARMESAN DRESSING

Great the next day—even better the next week!

1/2 cup buttermilk
1/2 cup nonfat mayonnaise
1   small onion, finely chopped
1   teaspoon Dijon mustard
1   tablespoon fresh lemon juice
1/3 teaspoon black pepper
1   garlic clove, minced
4   tablespoons Parmesan cheese
*   additional black pepper to taste*
*   additional Parmesan cheese to taste*

Thoroughly mix all salad ingredients in a bowl. Just before serving, toss dressing with salad. Sprinkle additional Parmesan cheese and black pepper over each portion of salad.

Store dressing in a covered jar or airtight container in the refrigerator.

SERVES 8.

DOM'S QUICKY SALAD DRESSING

Okay, listen.

When you don't have a salad dressing and your company is ready, put your chilled greens, onions, tomatoes, cucumbers, radishes, mushrooms, black olives, celery, whatever, in a bowl that has been rubbed with a cut garlic clove. Add...

1/3 cup olive oil
*   pepper to taste*
1/2 teaspoon sugar
*   juice of one lemon*
2   tablespoons vinegar
1/2 teaspoon oregano

Toss with salad spoons, sprinkle the top with a little Parmesan cheese, and serve it with no shame.

YIELDS ABOUT $^1\!/_2$ CUP.

WHITE BEAN AND TUNA SALAD

Even better tomorrow!

2	*15-oz. cans cannellini, white beans, kidney beans or navy beans, drain one can*
$^1\!/_3$	*cup olive oil*
2	*tablespoons lemon juice*
	freshly ground black pepper
2	*tablespoons chopped parsley*
2	*7-oz. cans white solid tuna, drained*
1	*medium onion, chopped*
2	*stalks celery, diced*
2	*teaspoons capers*
2 or 3	*chopped basil leaves*
8	*cherry tomatoes*
	basil leaves

Place beans in a large bowl. Add olive oil, lemon juice, pepper, parsley, tuna, onion, celery, capers and chopped basil. Gently mix everything together, garnish with fresh basil leaves and cherry tomatoes and serve.

SERVES 8–10.

GARDEN PASTA SALAD

Good after the company has gone home!

1   *10-oz. can drained artichoke hearts*

1/2   *pound cooked spiral or corkscrew noodles*

8–10   *cooked asparagus spears, cut into 2-inch pieces and lightly steamed*

6–8   *mushrooms, sliced*

1   *small red onion, chopped*

1   *small red bell pepper, chopped*

1   *6-oz. can black pitted olives, drained*

2   *tablespoons grated cheese*

1   *tablespoon cider vinegar*

8   *tablespoons olive oil and the juice of one lemon (or 1/4 cup Italian salad dressing)*

1   *teaspoon sugar*

1   *tablespoon capers*
        pepper to taste

3   *cups torn leaf lettuce*

Cut each artichoke heart into four pieces. In a serving bowl, combine the artichoke hearts with the remaining ingredients, except lettuce. Marinate for 30 minutes in the refrigerator.

Serve on lettuce.

SERVES 4–6.

ASPARAGUS, SHRIMP AND MUSHROOM SALAD

1   pound thin green asparagus, cut into 1½-inch pieces
     chicken broth
1   pound medium shrimp, shelled and deveined
1   tomato, diced
12   medium mushrooms, sliced
2   stalks celery, chopped
1   small onion, chopped

DRESSING:
2   tablespoons olive oil
     juice of one lemon
     pepper to taste
1   tablespoon minced parsley
¼   teaspoon thyme
2   tablespoons capers

Drop asparagus in boiling chicken broth for 1 minute until asparagus is just done. Do not overcook. Remove asparagus, set aside. Bring the cooking liquid back to a boil. Add shrimp and cook for 1 minute. Remove shrimp and set aside.

In a bowl add oil, lemon juice, pepper, parsley, thyme and capers. Mix and add tomato, mushrooms, onion, celery, asparagus and shrimp. Mix gently.

Refrigerate for about 2 hours. Serve on bed of lettuce with lemon wedges.

Great for a buffet!

SERVES 10–15.

ITALIAN SEAFOOD SALAD

1   *pound cooked squid, cleaned and rinsed thoroughly, pouches
     cut into rings, triangular fins sliced into strips, and tentacles
     left whole*
1   *pound shrimp, cooked, peeled and deveined*
1   *onion, chopped*
4   *tablespoons capers*
2   *large stalks celery, halved lengthwise and chopped*
4   *cups shredded lettuce*
1   *red onion, thinly sliced*
     lemon wedges

MARINADE:

1¹/₂   *tablespoons virgin olive oil*
1   *onion, chopped*
4   *garlic cloves, crushed*
       juice of one lemon
4   *tablespoons chopped parsley*
       pepper to taste

Put the squid, shrimp, onions, capers and celery into a large bowl, add
the marinade. Cover the mixture and place in the refrigerator to marinate
for at least 2 hours.

Just before serving, mix 2 cups shredded lettuce into the seafood.
Serve on a bed of shredded lettuce, garnish with a few red onion rings and
lemon wedges.

SERVES 8–10.

SALMON OR SHRIMP PASTA SALAD

Great for lunch.

1	*pound pasta (spirals or ziti)*
2	*stalks celery, chopped*
4	*tablespoons tarragon leaves, minced*
4	*tablespoons minced scallion*
1	*cup peas (fresh or frozen)*
4	*tablespoons lemon juice*
1	*cup nonfat mayonnaise pepper to taste*
1	*pound shrimp, cooked (for about 1½ minutes), cleaned and deveined (or 1 pound salmon that has been broiled or poached and skin and bones removed. Break into flakes.)*
12	*cherry tomatoes cut in half*
12	*lettuce leaves*

Cook pasta al dente and set aside. Mix celery, tarragon, scallion, peas, lemon juice, mayonnaise, pepper and half of the cherry tomatoes in a large bowl. Add the pasta and toss until well coated. Add the shrimp and stir gently.

Serve on lettuce and garnish with the other half of the cut cherry tomatoes.

A hot loaf of crusty Italian bread would complete the picture.

SERVES 6–8.

Ron Moody

*T*his is a picture of me and the amazingly talented Ron Moody, who won an Academy Award for the role of Fagin in *Oliver* and was also in Mel Brooks's *The Twelve Chairs*. Ron was a lot of fun, as was Mel Brooks and Frank Langella, who is an awesome actor. Frank and I have been friends for forever, it seems. We've had some good laughs. When I took this picture, I remember that I was there but it seems like another lifetime ago.

GREEK SALAD WITH BAY SHRIMP AND SQUID RINGS

Ah, Greece!

2   *stalks celery, chopped*
1   *medium cucumber, peeled and coarsely chopped*
2   *medium tomatoes, coarsely chopped*
1   *green pepper, chopped*
1   *medium red onion, thinly sliced*
1/2 *cup Greek black olives*
6   *tablespoons red wine vinegar*
8   *tablespoons olive oil*
    juice from one lemon
2   *teaspoons oregano*
    pepper to taste
1   *pound each of bay shrimp and squid rings*
4   *ounces feta cheese, crumbled*
    lemon wedges

Mix celery, cucumber, tomatoes, green pepper, onion and olives together in a large bowl. Add vinegar, olive oil, lemon juice, oregano and pepper. Mix well.

Bay Shrimp: Drop in boiling water for about 1 minute, just until they turn pink. Drain and set aside.

Squid: Boil water in a medium pan. Add squid rings and cook briefly, about 30 seconds. The squid is done when it turns white. Drain well. Place shrimp and squid rings in the bowl with the dressing. Mix gently. Sprinkle with feta cheese and chill about 1 hour before serving. Serve with lemon wedges.

SERVES 8–12.

I love this salad so much, I really am ashamed of myself because whenever I am eating it I don't take the time to acknowledge that there might be other people in the room!

I hope you like it too.

Soup

CHICKEN SOUP

It wouldn't hurt!

whole chicken, 2 or 3 pounds, skin removed
about 3–4 quarts water
3 *potatoes, peeled and cut into eighths*
2 *onions, cut into eighths*
3 *stalks celery, cut into bite-size pieces*
1 *sweet potato, sliced*
4 *tablespoons minced parsley*
4 *carrots, peeled and cut into bite-size pieces*
3 *garlic cloves, minced*
2 *small tomatoes, cut into sixths*
6 *asparagus spears, cut into bite-size pieces*
   pepper to taste

Put chicken in a large pot and cover with water. Bring to a boil, cover, then cook over low heat for about 1 hour. Remove chicken, discard skin, fat and bones, then set chicken meat aside.

Put all the vegetables in the pot, cover and simmer another hour. Add chicken meat, cover and cook another 10 minutes. Add pepper to taste. Serve as a meal with bread and salad, and add grated nonfat cheese if you'd like. And serve it to anyone who might have a cold! It couldn't hurt!

SERVES 8–10.

LENTIL SOUP

When I was a kid, I didn't like this. Now, I love it soooo much. Stand back!

2   *cups lentils*
4   *cups chicken broth*
    water
2   *carrots, sliced*
1   *medium onion, chopped*
2   *stalks celery, chopped*
1   *12-oz. can tomato sauce*
3   *garlic cloves, chopped*
1   *tablespoon olive oil*
1   *teaspoon oregano*
    pepper to taste
1/2 cup grated nonfat cheese

In a large pot, put lentils, chicken broth and water (enough to cover 2 inches above lentils). Bring to a boil, then simmer for about 45 minutes. Add carrots, onion, celery and tomato sauce.

In a small saucepan, sauté garlic in olive oil. Add oil, garlic, oregano and pepper to the soup. Simmer 15 minutes more.

Top with grated cheese and serve with hot bread and salad. Add a squeeze of lemon juice to each serving.

Add any of the following to the lentils:

1   *15-oz. can kidney beans*
1   *cup cooked rice*
1   *cup cooked pasta (bow ties)*
1   *15-oz. can pinto beans*
1   *15-oz. can black-eyed peas*
1   *cup cooked kasha*
1   *15-oz. can lima beans*
1   *pound spinach, stems removed*

You think of something you like, take a chance!

SERVES 10–12.

DOM'S TURKEY CORN CHOWDER

1   *parsley sprig, chopped*
2   *large stalks celery, chopped*
2   *cups leftover cooked turkey*
4   *tablespoons butter*
1   *red pepper, diced*
1   *onion, chopped*
1/2 *teaspoon freshly ground black pepper*
1   *20-oz. can creamed corn*
1   *20-oz. can whole kernel corn*
2   *14-oz. cans chicken broth*

Place everything in a large pot and simmer for 1 hour. It's thick and you do need a small shovel to eat it!

A crisp fresh salad and hot corn bread will make you and your guests even happier. Enjoy!

SERVES 6–8.

CHICKEN ASPARAGUS SOUP

1   *pound asparagus*
1   *cup regular or nonfat milk*
2   *sprigs parsley*
1/8 *teaspoon pepper*
1/4 *teaspoon dry mustard*
1   *10 1/2-oz. can cream of chicken soup*
1   *cup half-and-half*

Cook asparagus until tender crisp and cut into 1 inch lengths. Place asparagus, milk, parsley, pepper and dry mustard in blender container. Cover and blend for 30 seconds. Return to saucepan in which asparagus was cooked. Add chicken soup and half-and-half and stir in with wooden spoon or rotary beater.

Serve hot or cold with hot French bread.

SERVES 6.

NEW ENGLAND CLAM CHOWDER

3   garlic cloves, chopped
2   teaspoons olive oil
2   medium onions, chopped
3   potatoes, cubed
1/4 teaspoon pepper
2   cups chicken and broth
4   teaspoons flour
1   quart nonfat milk
2   tablespoons butter or margarine
1   28-oz. can chopped clams, with liquid

Sauté garlic in oil in a large pot. Add chopped onions, potatoes, chicken, pepper and broth. Simmer until potatoes are tender. To the pot then add the milk into which the flour has been stirred (no lumps!). Add butter, then add can of chopped clams with juice. Simmer 5 minutes longer and serve with hot rolls and *big* napkins.

SERVES 8–10.

This is Leticia and Maria, who have helped me a lot! Thank you both! *Muchas gracias!*

Dom DeLuise and Bob Newhart

There was a show in the '60s called "The Entertainers." It was a writers' show and in black-and-white. The show starred Carol Burnett, Caterina Valente and Bob Newhart. The newcomers on the show were John Davidson and me. It was great working with Bob. He was as kind then as he is now. I remember one Christmas he presented me with an attaché case that was the first I had ever gotten, and I was bowled over by his generosity. He sure is funny, and he worked for a year with my dear, sweet, talented friend, Suzanne Pleshette. Bob seems to go from series to series with what seems to be a half break

between series number one and series number two. All his reruns prove
he is very skilled because they are easy to watch and have stayed funny
even today. Mr. Newhart is very prolific and hysterically funny.

I guess we all like to know that someone is a family man. Bob is a
family man, and every time I go to church I see him and his family there.
Bob is great friends with Don Rickles and they laugh like children
together. I really admire him, there's only one like him, and thank God
we got him.

ESCAROLE AND BEANS

Peasant dish fit for a king.

2   *garlic cloves, minced*
1   *small onion, chopped*
2   *tablespoons olive oil*
1   *head escarole, washed and cut into pieces*
1   *carrot, sliced*
1   *cup chicken broth*
1   *16-oz. can cannellini beans*
4   *tablespoons grated nonfat cheese*
1/2 *cup grated cheese*

Sauté garlic and onion in oil in a saucepan until translucent. Add escarole,
carrot and broth, bring to a boil, and simmer for 20 minutes. Add beans
(do not stir) and cook for another 5 minutes. Stir gently to mix, then
serve topped with grated cheese and a long hot loaf of crusty bread!

SERVES 4.

DOM'S CREOLE GUMBO

2 *pounds shrimp/scallops, lobster, or other seafood, shelled, cleaned and deveined*
3 *tablespoons olive oil*
1 *onion, chopped*
1 *carrot, sliced*
4 *cloves garlic, minced*
1 *28-oz. can tomatoes*
1 *6-oz. can tomato paste*
1 *red pepper and 1 green pepper, coarsely chopped*
1/2 *teaspoon cayenne pepper*
1 *teaspoon parsley*
1 *teaspoon paprika*
10 *mushrooms, sliced*
2 *bay leaves*
1 *teaspoon oregano*
1 *teaspoon thyme*
1/2 *teaspoon Tabasco sauce*
12 *fresh okra, sliced*
2 *zucchini, sliced*
1 *stalk celery, chopped*
3 *tablespoons flour mixed with 1/2 cup cold water*

In a large pot sauté onion, carrot, and garlic in oil, until golden brown, then add all the remaining ingredients except the seafood. Cook over medium-low heat until flavors intermingle, about 30 minutes. Now add shrimp/scallops, mussels, clams, crabmeat or lobster. Cook just a few minutes until seafood is just done. Serve while still tender.

Serve over rice.

SERVES 8–12.

MANHATTAN CLAM CHOWDER

2   tablespoons olive oil
4   garlic cloves, minced
1   onion, chopped
1   green pepper, chopped
2   potatoes, peeled and diced
2   carrots, diced
2   stalks celery, diced
1   10-oz. can corn
1   28-oz. can crushed tomatoes
1   cup white wine
3   cups water
1/2   teaspoon oregano
1/4   teaspoon thyme
1/4   teaspoon pepper
2   teaspoons chopped fresh parsley
6   10-oz. cans minced clams (or 4 pounds fresh clams) with juice

Sauté garlic and onion in olive oil until golden brown. Add all other ingredients except clams.

Stir, bring to a boil, then reduce to a simmer for 1 hour. Fifteen minutes before serving add clams.

Serve with hot bread to dunk in the sauce.

SERVES 10–12.

Omelets
and Eggs

FRITTATA

A frittata and Julia Child, you are set!

Recently there was a survey taken by the Association of Grocery Store Owners. They asked the question: Whose refrigerator do you want to look into? I was the top man selected. I was really very flattered. The top women were Oprah Winfrey and Julia Child. I am completely crazy about Oprah and Julia. Julia of course is God. I will never forget the time we made a frittata together and as we broke the eggs, we threw the shells wildly over our shoulders. I have patterned my whole kitchen life after Julia's.

1/2	teaspoon olive oil
2	garlic cloves, minced
1	onion, chopped
1	red pepper, chopped
4–6	mushrooms, sliced
4	eggs (or egg equivalent)
2	tablespoons grated cheese

Add oil to a Teflon pan. Sauté garlic, onion, pepper and mushrooms till limp, about 5 minutes. In a bowl, beat eggs and grated cheese. Add vegetables to bowl. Mix eggs with vegetables.

Spray the pan with olive-oil spray and reheat. Add the egg mixture and cook for about 8 minutes on low. Turn once by putting a plate over the pan, turn pan and plate over, then slip frittata back in pan. Cook on the other side for an additional 1 or 2 minutes, then serve.

SERVES 2.

ALTERNATIVE I: Cook top of frittata by sliding uncovered pan under the broiler for 2 minutes. When you use this method you can add a slice of any of your favorite cheese. When cheese bubbles a little, remove from broiler, slide onto a plate and enjoy!

ALTERNATIVE II:
4 eggs or
1 egg and 3 egg whites or
4 egg equivalent

Note: This peasant dish was created by Italians to consume leftovers. If the pot roast was gone they would use the leftover vegetables to make a frittata. You can add leftover baked potato (diced), peas, meat, sausage, cooked carrots, leftover spinach or asparagus. Go crazy!

ARTICHOKE OMELET

Breakfast, lunch or dinner.

1/2 teaspoon olive oil
1   8-oz. jar artichoke hearts, drained
3   eggs (or 1 egg yolk and 3 egg whites), beaten (or egg equivalent)
2   ounces nonfat mozzarella cheese, sliced
*   pepper to taste*

FOR GARNISH:
tomato sauce
fresh basil leaves
tomato slices
cottage cheese

Heat olive oil in a 9-inch Teflon pan. Briefly sauté the artichoke hearts. In a bowl mix beaten eggs, cheese, pepper and artichokes. Reheat sprayed Teflon pan, add mixture, and cook over low heat about 8 minutes. Place plate over pan, flip omelet onto plate and flip back into pan to cook the other side. Cook 50 seconds more.

Garnish with tomato sauce, fresh basil, sliced tomato and more cheese.

SERVES 1.

Note: Replace artichokes with asparagus or spinach or mushrooms or red and green peppers or sausage or any combination. Anything you think you'd like in it will probably be terrific. Be brave. Go for it!

ESTELLE REINER'S WEST COAST MATZO BREI

"The Dick Van Dyke Show" was on the air for five glorious years. The man who created it was Carl Reiner, a man who has kept us laughing in so many different ways for so many years. Carl has been married to Estelle forever. Seems like we have been friends for just as long. He was in the right place at the right time when television exploded into a unique live happening called "Your Show of Shows" with Sid Caesar, Imogene Coca and Howie Morris, which was watched every Saturday night for a glorious hour and a half. The show was written by not only Sid Caesar and Carl Reiner, but Larry Gelbart, Neil Simon, Michael Stewart and the uncontrollable and wild Mel Brooks, whose middle name is "spontaneous" and who, along with Carl Reiner, made comic history with their innovative and delicious "Two Thousand Year Old Man." They subsequently made a second recording when the Man was 2037, a recording session I had the privilege of being at with my wife and kids. We were also lucky enough to be at their latest recording in 1997.

Carl and Estelle are warm, wonderful, funny people who care a great deal about their family and the human spirit. They love to eat and laugh and are really great hosts. Together they made three children: Rob, who was so amusing as Meathead with Carroll O'Connor in "All in the Family," has developed into one of the finest film directors in the world. His track record is truly amazing. I did a picture called *Fatso* written and directed by Anne Bancroft. In it, I had the privilege of working with Estelle Reiner, who was so hysterical in a scene I did with her I lost control because I laughed so much (something I do very well).

Estelle is a jazz singer par excellence. I am personally crazy about her and obviously her son Rob is as well. When Rob directed *When Harry Met Sally*, a film in which he asked the leading lady, Meg Ryan, to fake an orgasm in a restaurant, it was Rob who selected Estelle Reiner, who was in real life his actual mother, to respond to a waiter's question, "Can I help you ma'am?" with, "I'll have what she's having." The biggest laugh in the film! Go, Estelle!

Carl and Estelle also have a daughter named Annie who is a brilliant psychiatrist. I was in New York in great need of some help. I got in touch with Annie Reiner. She made lots of phone calls, and my problem was on the way to being solved. I will always be grateful to her for that.

The Reiners also created Lucas, who is married to Maude, with a beautiful baby named Livia. Lucas is a gifted painter. Estelle and Annie paint as well, but Lucas seems to have run with it. I truly admire their entire family—they are loving, creative, talented and risk-takers—every one.

I recently asked Estelle to help me with a matzo brei recipe. Estelle is one of the great cooks of all time! Eating food from her table was so good that if I was going to the electric chair, I would be satisfied with Estelle's cooking for my last meal. When I called Estelle for the matzo brei recipe, I was very surprised when she said, "As Jewish as I am, I never made matzo brei in my life." I was surprised because I think of her as the all-knowing Estelle. Half an hour later she called me up with a recipe for it. Fifteen minutes later she called to say "you can also add sautéed onions." Five minutes later she called again. "Or if you want you can sprinkle cinnamon while it's cooking." Oh how I love that woman! I mentioned that Estelle paints. I have a gorgeous painting she did in an impressionistic style of a Renaissance man lying down. I love this picture. It is hanging in my bathroom so I get to see it five or six times a day whether I want to or not.

Here's the matzo brei recipe from my friend Estelle.

4 *regular matzo*
4 *eggs*
2 *tablespoons oil*
1 *onion, minced (optional)*

Soak broken matzo in warm water for 2 to 3 minutes. Drain. Put drained matzo and eggs in a bowl and mix. Put oil in a Teflon pan and heat to hot (if using onion, brown them first). Put the matzo and eggs in the frying pan, mixing until the eggs are firm.

SERVES 2–4.

MATZO BREI FROM CANTOR ALAN EDWARDS

Lots of people tell you about when they were growing up and how they loved matzo brei.

Michael, who works for me, called his father, Cantor Alan Edwards, because I wanted to ask him for the recipe. When he said he put wine in it I said, "Wait, wait. Who told you to put wine in the matzo brei?" He said, "Nobody. It was my idea. I just like the flavor of wine." I *tried* this and it worked good. Of course the next day I went out and bought concord grape wine. I'm no fool. It does taste exotic and very delicious. So for years now I don't make matzo brei without wine. If you ask me who told me to put wine in my matzo brei, I will say Cantor Edwards from Philadelphia, U.S.A. This one is different and oh so good!

4   *regular matzo*
2   *tablespoons oil*
3   *eggs or egg equivalent*
1/2 *cup milk*
6–8 *teaspoons sugar*
1/2 *cup sweet grape wine, such as Maneschewitz*

Soak broken matzo in warm water for 2 to 3 minutes. Drain. Put oil in a Teflon pan and heat to hot, put drained matzo in pan and stir constantly. Mix eggs, milk, and sugar in a glass bowl. Add to the pan while mixing matzo, then slowly add wine. Keep mixing until eggs are firm.

SERVES 2–4.

POACHED EGGS IN TOMATO SAUCE

My pop's favorite. Mine too!

2   *garlic cloves, chopped*
1   *medium onion, chopped*
1/2 teaspoon olive oil
1   *16-oz. can stewed tomatoes (or 1 pound peeled fresh tomatoes)*
     pepper to taste
8   *eggs*
     few basil leaves, chopped
     grated nonfat cheese

In a deep 9-inch frying pan, sauté the garlic and onion in olive oil. Add tomatoes and simmer 15 minutes on low heat. Add pepper to taste. Carefully drop eggs in sauce, cover, and poach for 3 minutes (no more) for soft eggs and about 5 minutes for hard eggs. Remove from heat and place the poached eggs in serving dishes. Spoon tomato sauce over eggs. Crown each serving with basil leaves, sprinkle with grated cheese, and serve with toasted Italian bread.

SERVES 6.

Note: Use some Tabasco sauce for an extra kick and a great big hot loaf of crusty bread.

Coney Island

W hen I was a little kid growing up in Brooklyn, my friends and I had to take a train to Coney Island. We would take a bathing suit, a towel, ten cents for the subway (that was for both ways) and my mother's pepper and egg sandwiches. Olive oil, garlic, green peppers and scrambled egg, piled into an Italian hero roll. When you sit on the train with this hot, wonderful-smelling sandwich, it can be so tempting! It was a miracle if the sandwich ever made it to Coney Island. It was supposed to be our lunch. Sometimes our whole family would go to Coney Island and we would go by subway because we didn't have a car. We'd take blankets and drinks and sandwiches. For some reason they were invariably peppers and eggs on

On the beach. This is my son David and his grandma, Vincenza DeStefano DeLuise.

Italian bread. There was nothing more comforting when you were
exhausted and wet after a couple of hours of being knocked about in the
ocean than having a giant towel thrown over your head and your mother
drying your hair as you munched on a pepper and egg sandwich, the
bread of which had already sopped up a lot of the flavor. There was just
enough sand blowing around on your fingers that not only was each bite
delicious and warm, but it also had a little crunch. I guess it was the smell
of the ocean, the egg, the comfort of having your mother there with
enough sandwiches to satisfy everybody, and her disposition to be completely satisfied drying your hair while you ate. I remember my mother in
a black bathing suit holding onto a rope that was put in the water so people could stand there and wade. It was great for a nonswimmer. My mother loved the ocean but she never swam. When she came to our home in
Los Angeles, she brought the bathing suit. She was eighty-five and went
into the pool. I asked her to please make her famous peppers and eggs on
rolls and of course she did. She was standing in my pool, saying, "Dom,
you live like a king." But it seems to me I was living like a king on Coney
Island with my friends, my family, my pepper and egg sandwiches and
with my hair being dried by my Mama Jenny. A towel crown would smell
so sweet!

Sauces
and Pasta

MARINARA SAUCE

Fast, fast and good, good, good!

4 *tablespoons olive oil*
5 *garlic cloves, minced*
1 *small onion, chopped*
8 *fresh basil leaves, chopped*
2 *tablespoons chopped parsley*
1 *6-oz. can tomato paste*
2 *28-oz. cans tomatoes*
1/2 *teaspoon oregano*
  pepper to taste

Pour olive oil in a large saucepan, and sauté garlic and onion until translucent. Add basil, parsley, tomato paste, tomatoes and oregano. Simmer for 20 minutes, then add pepper to taste. Serve on your choice of pasta or any dish needing marinara sauce—chicken, fish, veal, beef, vegetables, lasagne.

SERVES 4–6.

CATERINA VALENTE'S PUTTANESCA SAUCE (HARLOT SAUCE)

So good!

I have a very talented friend named Caterina Valente who has been my friend for a lot of years. We first met when we were both involved in a TV show that starred Carol Burnett, Bob Newhart and a very young John Davidson. We did lots of musical numbers. We spent all our rehearsing hours together with the singers and dancers. We would often get together for "gypsy dinners."

It was Caterina Valente who first made this "harlot" sauce for me and all the gypsies. ("Gypsies" is a theatrical term referring to all those hardworking singers and dancers in the show.) Caterina made an enormous pot of this incredible sauce, and I can remember there wasn't a drop left, which is a great testimony to its flavor and of course, her cooking ... even though everyone in the theater knows that gypsies will eat anything. God bless them, every one. Enjoy!

Me and Caterina dancing in "The Entertainers."

4   *garlic cloves, minced*
4   *tablespoons olive oil*
2   *28-oz. cans ready-cut tomatoes*
1   *16-oz. can pitted whole black olives, drained*
6   *tablespoons capers, with juice*
12 *fresh basil leaves, chopped*
    pinch of red pepper flakes
    pepper to taste
    grated cheese

Sauté garlic in the oil until golden brown. Add the tomatoes and simmer for 10 minutes. Add olives, capers, basil, red pepper and pepper. Simmer in an uncovered pot for 20 minutes, stirring gently until sauce has thickened. Serve on 1½ pound of pasta cooked al dente.

Serve with grated cheese and hot Italian bread and wine. Excellent for gypsies, harlots, starlets or just plain friends.

OPTIONAL: A small can of anchovies can be added to the sauce. This is very traditional. However, I don't use them.

SERVES 4–6.

DOM'S MEAT SAUCE

Meat sauce, your majesty?

2 *tablespoons olive oil*
4 *garlic cloves, minced*
2 *ounces prosciutto, chopped*
2 *onions, finely chopped*
2 *pounds lean beef, turkey, pork or veal (or any combination)*
1 *cup red wine*
1 *6-oz. can tomato paste*
2 *28-oz. cans chopped tomatoes (or 4 pounds peeled,*
    chopped tomatoes)
1 *teaspoon sugar*
   pepper to taste
1 *teaspoon oregano*
1 *cup fresh basil, cut up*

In a large saucepan over medium heat, add oil, garlic, prosciutto and onions. Sauté until translucent. Slowly add the ground meat of your choice, stirring with a wooden spoon until all the pink is gone and the meat is crumbly. Discard fat. Add wine, tomato paste, tomatoes, sugar, pepper and oregano and stir. Simmer for 1 hour.

Serve on your favorite pasta. I love to add pieces of fresh basil on each serving—the green and the red really work together...Woof!

SERVES 8.

PROSCIUTTO SAUCE

This recipe is great on mostaccioli, angel hair pasta or spaghetti. You can even add your favorite meatballs!

1 pound mostaccioli, ziti or penne
1 medium onion, finely chopped
3 tablespoons olive oil
3 slices prosciutto, chopped
4 tablespoons chopped fresh basil
1 28-oz. can crushed tomatoes
1 6-oz. can tomato paste
   pepper to taste
   grated cheese

Cook the pasta al dente. In a medium saucepan, sauté onion in oil until translucent, then add prosciutto and basil and cook for 2 or 3 minutes. Add crushed tomatoes and tomato paste and stir. Add pepper. Simmer for 1 hour. Serve over pasta with grated cheese.

   Fast and oh so good!

SERVES 4.

Mickey Rooney

I met Mickey Rooney many years ago when we were doing a play called *Luv* with Joan Rivers. The three of us were, if I do say so myself, hysterical. We were working for a wonderful man named John Kenley who was the head of The Kenley Players that had theaters in Warren, Dayton and Columbus, Ohio, and Flint, Michigan. I grew up seeing the famous, adorable, talented Mickey Rooney grow up on the screen, and here I was working on stage with him and Joan Rivers, and I was in heaven.

Mickey Rooney is one of the most talented men I've ever met in my entire life. If you look at television you can see how extremely talented he was starring at age eight in *Midsummer Night's Dream* to his present-day acting. When Sir Laurence Olivier was asked who, in his opinion, was the best American actor, he said without hesitation, "Mickey Rooney, of course." He is the most natural actor I have ever seen.

When my children were small, I took them to see Mickey in *Sugar Babies* with Ann Miller. He was hysterically funny in the show and he welcomed the entire DeLuise clan backstage. He was very entertaining in the dressing room. When our family went back to New York two months later, I asked the kids, "Is there anything you'd like to do while we're here in New York?" "Yeah, we want to see Mickey Rooney." "You mean, in *Sugar*

Babies again?" I asked. They said, "No, we want to see him backstage in his dressing room." Mickey gives great "Rooney."

I was in an opera in Los Angeles called *Orpheus in the Underworld* with a lot of very talented people.

Unfortunately, the show didn't get good reviews. The cast was a little stunned until I pinned on the bulletin board an enlarged version of a telegram I had received from Mickey. "Don't listen to the critics," he wrote. "You're all gifted by God, and you can enrich the world with your talent and skills. The critics only criticize. You enhance the world with your talent. You are truly blessed. Love, Mickey." I am paraphrasing a little bit, but that was the essence of his telegram. You should have seen the looks on the faces of all those talented people. At first, big grins, and then their lips pressed together, some halted breathing followed by moist and grateful eyes. Mickey has made a big difference in my life and I love the fact that I have known him since my son Peter was two years old. All my children love him because of the way he acted and behaved in his dressing room, and I'm grateful for the place that he has chiseled into my heart. Either way, Mickey is a winner. I had the privilege of working with him in a movie I directed called *Boys Will Be Boys,* and he was fabulous, of course. He just reacted to everything that happened to him in front of the camera spontaneously, differently every time, but always fresh and funny. Of course, in the one serious scene in the picture where Mickey had to bombard Randy Travis, his serious acting was flawless. Oh God, how I love that man! His instincts still reign. He celebrated his eightieth birthday with us and entertained us all for about twenty minutes.

He told a story about Walt Disney having lunch with a very young Mickey Rooney as a new cartoon mouse was about to be named. His name was supposed to be Mortimer or something, and the story goes that Mr. Disney said "How do you like this mouse called Mortimer, Mickey?" He says that Walt Disney's eyes flashed and he said, "Mick? Mortimer? Wait a minute. Mickey, how'd you like this new mouse to be named after you? How does it sound, Mickey? Mickey Mouse—Is that O.K. with you?" The young Mickey smiled, shook hands with Walt Disney, and said, "Mickey Mouse it is." Isn't it wonderful that this world was big enough for Mickey Rooney? My amazing friend Mickey Rooney.

PASTA WITH OIL, GARLIC AND NUTS

My favorite! Great the next day.

1	pound angel hair pasta
3–5	garlic cloves, minced
8–10	tablespoons olive oil
1/2	cup walnuts or pecans
1/2	cup pine nuts or sunflower seeds (or 1 cup of your favorite nut)
2	tablespoons chopped parsley
	pepper to taste
	fresh basil leaves
	grated nonfat cheese

Cook pasta al dente. In a large frying pan, sauté garlic in olive oil. Add walnuts, pine nuts and parsley. Add cooked pasta to frying pan. Immediately, while pasta is still hot, toss thoroughly. Add pepper to taste.

Garnish with a few fresh basil leaves. Serve with grated cheese and some white wine.

SERVES 4.

DOM'S PESTO SAUCE

I cook my garlic before!

12　*garlic cloves*
1/2　*cup olive oil*
1　*cup nuts (walnuts, pecans, pignoli)*
　　coarsely chopped
2　*cups fresh basil leaves*
1/2　*cup grated Parmesan cheese*

In a pan slowly, gently sauté the garlic in 2 tablespoons of the olive oil, till *golden* brown. Transfer garlic and oil to a blender and mix a little. Stop blending and then add basil, grated cheese and nuts. Blend for about 3 seconds so the nuts stay coarse. This works great on any al dente pasta. Add more grated Parmesan cheese to taste and go!

This sauce freezes like a charm!

SERVES 4–5 PEOPLE PER POUND OF PASTA.

That's me on top of the "Amazing" Joe and Mike (the Gugliotti Brothers) in "The Entertainers." I don't go that high anymore!

SAUSAGE TOMATO SAUCE

For those sausage lovers like my son Michael. I mean, if you give my son Michael sausage, he'll follow you anywhere.

2 garlic cloves, minced
1 small onion, minced
2 tablespoons olive oil
1 pound sweet Italian pork sausage (Turkey sausage is excellent too.)
1 28-oz. can tomatoes
3 tablespoons cut-up fresh basil
1 teaspoon thyme
   pepper to taste

In a large saucepan over medium heat, sauté garlic and onion in oil until translucent. Add sausage and brown slightly on both sides. Drain off fat if you use pork sausage. Add tomatoes, basil, thyme and pepper. Heat until sauce is bubbly, then reduce heat. Cover and simmer for 1 hour; 15 minutes for turkey or chicken.

Serve on pasta of your choice. Add fresh cut-up basil leaves and sprinkle with grated cheese.

SERVES 4–6.

DAILY NEWS
DOM DeLUISE KING OF BROOKLYN

Citation

That's me and my family, with me wearing my "King of Brooklyn" crown.

RUTH BUZZI'S QUICK—SIT DOWN! IT'LL BE READY IN A MINUTE—SAUCE

Ruth Buzzi and I met when we were working at Provincetown, Massachusetts, a hundred years ago. That's also where I first met my wife, Carol. In fact we were all in a show called *Summer and Smirk*. We have been friends all these years and Ruthie and my wife, Carol, have been very close and enjoy being two characters, Rose and Rita, girls who live by their wits on the streets of New York. They are both very strange and wonderfully funny pretending to be Rose and Rita. It's just for their own enjoyment, but an awful lot of the fun rubs off on Kent, Ruth's husband, and me.

Kent Perkins is a truly wonderful man with one impossible trait. He happens to play the piano very well and has even written some great songs that are touching and have been recorded. That part is great! However when he plays the piano he plays it so loud he breaks windows in nearby homes just with his sheer volume alone. He once played "Glory, Glory Hallelujah" so loud, three birds that were in flight midair, fell to the ground dead.

Anyway we were all together at their home in Bear Valley, California, and we were playing cards one night for hours and the next time we looked up it was too late to go out to dinner and Ruth actually said, "Sit down! It'll be ready in a minute!" and she started to make this dinner in about, well, it seemed like 15 minutes. I mean it was fast. I know we were hungry but we just went to town on a simple salad and this pasta dish coming up. I said, "Ruth, how did you know it would work?" She smiled and said, "I just trusted the Lord." Well, if it worked for Ruth, who we all know is a sinner (joke), it's bound to work for you. By the way, there were no leftovers.

Enjoy this quick, fast and gooood recipe!

Before you begin the sauce start a pot of water boiling...for the pasta!

1	*onion, minced*
1	*8-oz. jar pimentos, cut up (or 1 red pepper, diced)*
1	*tablespoon olive oil*
6–8	*mushrooms sliced (or 1 8-oz. jar sliced mushrooms, drained)*
1	*cup frozen petite peas (or 1 can peas, drained)*
1	*10½-oz. can cream of mushroom soup*
1	*tablespoon light soy sauce*
½	*teaspoon paprika*
	freshly ground pepper to taste
1	*9¼-oz. can solid white tuna rinsed, drained and broken up (or 8 ounces bay shrimp added at last minute)*
⅓	*cup white wine*
	fresh basil
2	*tablespoons grated cheese*
1	*pound rigatoni*

In a large Teflon pan sauté the onion (and red pepper if using fresh) and add all the other ingredients except the rigatoni. Stir gently with a wooden spoon and cook on low for a few minutes. Meanwhile you have thrown in the rigatoni. Cook al dente. Drain pasta and pour sauce over pasta. Mix gently. Top with fresh basil, more cracked pepper and grated cheese if you like. It's fast and these are items we all might have on a shelf. *N'est-ce pas?*

SERVES 4–5 PEOPLE PER POUND OF PASTA.

LASAGNE

One lasagne pan, assemble cold, no mess—perfect!

1	*pound lasagne noodles*
2	*quarts marinara sauce (or sauce of your choice)*
2	*pounds lowfat ricotta cheese*
1	*pound lowfat mozzarella cheese, thinly sliced or grated*
1	*cup grated Parmesan cheese*
6–8	*mushrooms, thinly sliced*

Do not cook lasagne noodles. Assemble everything cold.

Using a baking dish, cover the bottom with sauce and line with a layer of lasagne. Dot with spoonfuls of ricotta, slices of mozzarella and grated Parmesan cheese. Cover with a layer of sauce. Top this layer with sliced mushrooms. Repeat with another layer of lasagne and cheeses until dish is almost filled. Top with sauce and a sprinkling of grated cheese. (I dip my cold lasagne noodles in my cold pasta sauce just before I make the layers.) Cover and bake at 325 degrees about 45 minutes. Lasagne is done when a knife goes straight down to the bottom of the pan easily. Remove from oven and allow to sit 20 minutes before serving. Serve with additional sauce.

SERVES 6–8.

OPTIONAL: You can add spinach, sliced meatballs or sliced cooked sausage to one of the layers of the lasagne.

LUCY'S PASTA

When I was a kid in Brooklyn, our neighbor, Lucy, was like a second mother to me. She taught me how to make this dish when I was fourteen and very impressionable.

God Bless you, Mamma Lucy! I am always pleased with this dish.

5   *garlic cloves, minced*
1/3 *cup olive oil*
3   *onions, sliced into thin crescents*
1   *pound spaghetti or linguine*
3   *eggs*
1/2 *cup fresh parsley, finely chopped*
1/2 *cup grated cheese*
1   *cup fresh basil, cut into small pieces*
     ground pepper to taste

In a medium frying pan cook garlic in olive oil over medium heat. Add onions and sauté gently until golden brown. Cook pasta al dente. While pasta cooks, beat together eggs, half the parsley, half the grated cheese, half the basil and pepper in a large serving bowl. Drain pasta (do not rinse) and place while very hot in the bowl with the egg mixture. Toss gently. The heat from the pasta will cook the eggs. Add contents of frying pan, then mix with pasta, the remaining basil, parsley, pepper and grated cheese.

Enjoy with good wine and a friend. Great the next day!

SERVES 4–5.

PASTA WITH RICOTTA

When I went to visit my niece Concetta, who's an optometrist and lives in Boston, she improvised a pasta lunch and I was very impressed. It's got just four ingredients but it is really wonderful. The pasta was very al dente and the creamy texture of the ricotta combined beautifully with the Parmesan cheese and the black pepper and I was hooked. Later in that same meal she introduced me to plum sauce and some other Chinese seasonings and I knew that I couldn't trifle with my niece Concetta. Years later when she adopted a little Chinese girl I knew she meant business. I learned a lot of things from my niece besides cooking—how to love unselfishly and how to celebrate life. I'm saying all this because if she reads it I'm sure she'll send me a free pair of glasses.

This is one of the simplest recipes you'll ever see and a taste you won't forget.

olive-oil spray
1 *pound long fusille*
2 *cups ricotta cheese*
fresh cracked black pepper
grated Parmesan cheese

Serve in a large bowl that has been sprayed with olive oil. Add drained pasta cooked al dente, ricotta, black pepper and cheese. Stir gently, re-cheese and eat!

SERVES 4–5 PEOPLE PER POUND OF PASTA.

DOM'S RIGATONI AND BROCCOLI 2

1   *pound rigatoni or mostaccioli*
2   *cups broccoli florets*
4   *tablespoons olive oil*
1   *teaspoon flour*
3/4   *cup cold nonfat milk*
1   *cup shredded nonfat mozzarella or Monterey Jack cheese*
      pepper to taste
      nonfat grated cheese

To a pot of boiling water, add the rigatoni and 2 minutes later add the broccoli. Cook another 3 minutes. While still al dente, drain the pasta and broccoli and pour into a large serving bowl. While the pasta and broccoli are cooking, add oil to a saucepan. Add flour to the cold milk and mix thoroughly until smooth and without lumps. Add the milk and flour to the oil in saucepan and stir over medium heat with wooden spoon until the sauce thickens. Add cheese to sauce, stir briefly, and immediately pour over the pasta and broccoli. Stir gently. Serve.

Add pepper to taste, and grated cheese if you like.

SERVES 4.

Note: Instead of the oil, flour, milk, replace all that with a can of cream of mushroom soup. It will do the job and you will have one less pot to clean.... Get it?

PASTA WITH MOZZARELLA AND 20-MINUTE GARDEN FRESH TOMATO SAUCE

6   *large tomatoes (3 or 4 pounds)*
2   *garlic cloves, minced*
3   *tablespoons olive oil*
1   *cup fresh basil leaves*
1/2 *cup fresh parsley*
    pepper to taste
1   *pound fusille, rotini or your favorite pasta*
3/4 *pound grated mozzarella cheese*

Magic trick to peel tomatoes: boil a pot of water, drop tomatoes in boiling water for 10 seconds, then easily peel. Coarsely chop tomatoes. In a large saucepan, lightly brown garlic in the olive oil. Add chopped tomatoes, basil and parsley. Cook over medium heat for approximately 10 minutes. Add pepper to taste. While the tomatoes are cooking, cook the pasta al dente (do not overcook). Place cooked pasta in a large serving bowl. Pour the chopped mozzarella and cooked tomatoes over the pasta. Mix thoroughly and serve.

SERVES 4–5.

RICOTTA GNOCCHI

These are lighter than the traditional potato gnocchi. I prefer these!

2 cups flour
2 eggs
2 cups ricotta
2 cups marinara sauce
  Parmesan cheese

Put the flour, eggs and ricotta in a mixing bowl. Blend with a wooden spoon. Mix with hands until dough is well blended and soft. With floured fingers, roll the dough into long cylindrical shapes about the width of your thumb. Cut the dough into pieces approximately 1 inch long. Press your fingertip in each piece, and curve the pieces of dough lengthwise into the shape of a shell. Using a large pot bring water to a boil. Drop gnocchi in boiling water and cook until they rise to the surface. Lift from water using strainer. Set the gnocchi in a bowl. Add marinara sauce and Parmesan cheese and serve piping hot.

SERVES 4.

PASTA WITH HORSERADISH OR "EAT IT AND WEEP!"

Once when I was a kid I saw my father eating pasta and crying so much I thought our dog had died. It was fresh horseradish on pasta. I thought he was out of his mind. Now I am all grown up and I love horseradish on my gefilte fish and once in a blue moon I enjoy it on my pasta.

cooked pasta
marinara sauce
freshly grated horse-
radish
freshly grated Parmesan
cheese
freshly ground black
pepper

Add to a dish of al dente pasta with light marinara sauce. Sprinkle on 2–4 tablespoons freshly grated horseradish. Mix gently and add freshly grated Parmesan cheese and fresh-ly ground pepper. You will weep as you consume this dish.

If you don't try it you can never know how my father felt.

DOM'S FRIEND EVE'S LUCKCHEN KUGEL

I have known and loved Eve Roberts for only 100 years. I love her like the sister I have. Carol and I share her—Carol loves her too! Eve makes this here kugel all the time—thank God!

This is *simpler* and different than your other kugels. Try it, you'll like it. Great for a buffet party.

5   eggs (or egg equivalent)
1/2 cup melted margarine
1   cup orange juice, milk, sweet wine or apple cider
1   cup sugar
1   teaspoon vanilla
1   cup peeled, diced apple and/or 1/2 cup raisins soaked and
     drained, or 1/2 cup chopped almonds
1   teaspoon cinnamon
1   pound wide noodles, cooked al dente and drained

Beat eggs together in a bowl, then add the rest of the ingredients (except cinnamon and noodles). Grease a glass dish and put in drained noodles.

Pour mixture over noodles, stir. Sprinkle top with cinnamon and bake in 350-degree oven for 1 hour.

There is nothing like this dish. It's a starch, it's almost a dessert and you can have it whenever you want. Just call it what you will. Breakfast, lunch, main meal, snack, pick-me-up!

And this will keep if there is any left

SERVES 4–6.

Note: Dorothy Paul is a very good friend of mine and a terrific casting director. She and I worked together on a movie I directed called *Boys Will Be Boys,* produced by her son Stephan, who is terrific. She was a great energetic boost to the whole project. She and her husband Hank and I were having a very serious discussion one day about noodle kugel and when I told her about the recipe I had with sugar and orange juice, she said: Me? I don't use sugar or orange juice at all. I use:

1 cup peeled and diced apple
1 cup raisins, soaked and drained

She said, "Use lots of butter. Remember, that's important. It'll kill you but you'll die happy!"

It cuts like a cake and comes out in a square. I made it her way and it was great. *No* leftovers. Need I say more!

Chicken and Turkey

CHICKEN PARMIGIANA

This also works great with veal, turkey, beef, pork or eggplant.

4   *skinless, boneless chicken breasts*
2   *eggs, beaten*
1   *cup seasoned bread crumbs*
    olive-oil spray
1   *cup marinara sauce*
1/2 *cup shredded mozzarella cheese*
    nonfat grated cheese

Cut chicken breasts into 1-inch squares. Cover with waxed paper, and pound until thin, about 1/4 inch. Dip in beaten eggs, then dip in bread crumbs. Spray a Teflon frying pan lightly with olive-oil spray and brown the breaded chicken on both sides. Place chicken in a baking dish. Add marinara sauce, and sprinkle cheeses on top.

Bake at 300 degrees for 10 minutes, or until cheese melts.

Serve with mashed potatoes or rice, or serve with your favorite pasta, in which case you'll need more marinara sauce. Maybe some steamed broccoli, and I think a crispy salad to top it off.

SERVES 4.

CHICKEN CACCIATORE

Better the next day!

1 whole chicken, cut up
and skin removed
(also perfect for rab-
bit, large veal pieces
or 2 skinless turkey
thighs)
2 carrots, cut into
pieces
1 red pepper, cut into
pieces
1 green pepper, cut
into pieces
1 medium onion,
sliced into crescents
8 mushrooms,
quartered
2 tablespoons olive
oil
1 teaspoon oregano
2 garlic cloves,
minced
1 tablespoon chopped parsley
1 cup wine (red or white)
1 10-oz. can stewed tomatoes

Carol and me cutting the cake at our wedding. That's my aunt Anna back there!

Place chicken pieces in a shallow baking dish. Arrange carrots, peppers, onion and mushrooms around chicken. Sprinkle with olive oil, oregano, garlic and parsley. Pour wine and stewed tomatoes over chicken, cover with foil, and bake at 300 degrees for 1½ hours.

Serve with potatoes, pasta or rice and maybe broccoli with hot bread and salad.

SERVES 4–6.

Frank Sinatra

Through the years I have been privileged to work with Frank Sinatra. When Burt Reynolds and I did *Cannonball Run*, Frank joined our cast. I remember he arrived by helicopter. We all went out to meet him— Burt, Dean Martin, Sammy Davis, Jr., Shirley MacLaine, Marilu Henner, and myself. There was a red carpet from the helicopter landing to make-up. The atmosphere changes when Frank's around, especially on a movie set. Everyone in the world comes out of the woodwork to meet The King. I remember Tony Danza was there with his son. Tony was a cast member of *Cannonball II* and he was so excited about the possibility of meeting Mr. Sinatra that when I said, "Frank, this is Tony Danza, Tony this is Frank," a giant smile fixed on Tony's face as he shook hands with Frank, who was as gracious as any man I have ever seen. That led to an introduction to Tony's then very young son. I know Frank is a celebrity among

celebrities and I could see that the security guards, there to protect him, were all lined up to take pictures with him. And, of course, he graciously obliged everyone. I never saw so many security guards so obediently in line in my life. After Frank had left, Tony Danza came over to me, grabbed my hand, and said, "Gee, thanks Dom. For me that's a dream come true." They have become very good friends since then!

Carol and I have spent some very precious time with Frank and Barbara, who is as warm and giving as she is beautiful. It doesn't take a rocket scientist to see how much in love they are. Barbara has a fantastic sense of humor and she is great company. She and Frank are wonderful hosts. She has the incredible ability to make you feel very special in her presence. She does a lot of important work for her charity—the Barbara Sinatra Children's Center at Eisenhower in Rancho Mirage—and has a celebrity cookbook called *Sinatra's Celebrity Cookbook* that has become extremely popular. When Frank, Barbara, Carol and I, along with Angie Dickinson and Pat and Larry Gelbart, play cards together, we all have a ball. Barbara serves hors d'oeuvres that are so hot, after you eat them you gasp for air and tears come to your eyes, which is great for me 'cause I

That's Jim Nabors, Shirley MacLaine, Burt Reynolds, Marilu Henner and me from *Cannonball II.*

love to cry. It was after eating just three that I was sobbing uncontrollably, and I knew Barbara and I could be "friends." To me, she will always be the Queen of Hearts.

When Barbara, Frank, Carol and I get together and his records are playing, I am especially aware of his Herculean contribution to the music world and I am humbled. And when he reminisces about his movie career, it unfolds like vivid pages of cinema history right before your eyes. . . . It's awesome. Then he says something about his beginnings, about being a street kid who made it big, making you feel very comfortable in his presence. Frank is the Amazing King who wears his crown unmistakably tilted toward the streets from where he came. Oh I have such respect and love for him!

FIT FOR A KING

Good enough for Frank himself, old blue eyes!

1   *whole chicken, 3 or 4 pounds*
2   *tablespoons olive oil*
4   *garlic cloves minced*
4   *potatoes with skin, quartered*
2   *onions, sliced into crescents*
2   *stalks celery, cut into pieces*
4   *carrots, cut into pieces*
1   *pound turkey (or pork) sausage*
1/2 *teaspoon oregano*
    pepper to taste

Rub chicken inside and out with olive oil. Place chicken in a large roasting pan, then sprinkle with garlic. Arrange potatoes, onions, celery, carrots and sausage around chicken. Sprinkle with oregano and pepper. Bake, uncovered, at 400 degrees for 1 hour and 15 minutes.

Serve with additional vegetables, potatoes and pan juice. Oh, and a big salad!

SERVES 6–8.

CHICKEN BREAST BRACIOLE

Can be done with veal, pork or beef, too.

2   *skinless, boneless chicken breasts*
1/2 *cup bread crumbs*
1/4 *pound nonfat mozzarella*
2   *tablespoons parsley*
2   *tablespoons olive oil*
2   *garlic cloves, minced*
4   *tablespoons wine*
     juice of one lemon

Cut each chicken breast into four pieces. Place chicken breasts between waxed paper and pound with a mallet until they are about $1/4$ inch thick. In the center of each piece place bread crumbs, mozzarella and parsley. Roll and secure with toothpicks.

In a frying pan over medium heat, sauté rolled chicken in olive oil and garlic for a few minutes until golden brown. Add wine, reduce heat, cover and cook 5 to 6 minutes.

Sprinkle with lemon juice and serve immediately.

SERVES 2.

LEMON CHICKEN WITH ALMONDS

4   *skinless, boneless chicken beast halves (also good with turkey)*
3   *tablespoons flour*
4   *tablespoons olive oil*
2   *garlic cloves, minced*
1/2 *cup chopped scallions*
1   *cup chicken broth*
1   *tablespoon fresh lemon juice*
1/2 *teaspoon grated lemon zest*
2   *tablespoons chopped fresh parsley*
4   *tablespoons sliced almonds, toasted*

Set each piece of chicken between two pieces of wax paper and pound with meat mallet or heavy-bottomed pan in order to flatten to 1/4 inch thick.

Coat each piece of chicken with flour. Using a nonstick skillet, sauté garlic in 3 tablespoons of olive oil. Sauté chicken in the skillet and cook over medium heat 2 minutes on each side, until color is golden brown and meat is no longer pink inside. Remove chicken and keep warm. Add 1 tablespoon olive oil and scallions to skillet and sauté over medium heat for 3 minutes. Mix in broth, lemon juice and lemon zest and bring to a boil. Simmer about 5 minutes until slightly thickened, scraping sides of skillet from time to time.

Spoon sauce over chicken. Garnish with parsley and almonds. Serve with mashed or baked potatoes and a green vegetable.

SERVES 4.

OPTIONAL: For something different, substitute 2 tablespoons capers for the almonds.

Me, James Williams and Jon during the filming of *Boys Will Be Boys*.

Jon Voight

I had the good fortune of directing a movie called *Boys Will Be Boys* with Randy Travis, Julie Hagerty, Mickey Rooney, Michael DeLuise, Kathleen Oxenberg, Charles Nelson Reilly and Ruth Buzzi, as well as two of the most talented young people I have ever had the good fortune to work with, James Williams and Drew Winget. I'm sure they are going to reach fantastic heights with their careers. James and Drew were brave, talented, and I shall never forget my experience with them. (James's mom and dad, Joni and Don, are both wonderful people. Joni makes great cookies and Don is a butcher. We were destined to be friends.) The whole experience was good, better, best. Jon Voight enhanced our film by playing a detective who, in the film, was going to slowly unravel our comic plot. I think Jon Voight is an amazing actor and I have admired him for years. He's a good friend of mine and I cherish his dedication, his talent, his loyalty, and probably most of all, his kooky humor. Things are better when Jon walks into a room. My whole existence was improved when he walked into my life. Jon keeps improving as a human being . . . and as a movie actor, I guess the sky's the limit.

DICED CHICKEN WITH WALNUTS

Chicken never had it so good!

3/4 *cup chicken broth*
1   *tablespoon cornstarch or flour*
2   *tablespoons light soy sauce*
4   *tablespoons white wine*
5   *tablespoons brown sugar*
4   *tablespoons peanut oil*
2   *whole chicken breasts, cut up to the size of half a walnut*
3   *medium onions, coarsely chopped*
1   *red pepper, cut into 1-inch pieces*
1   *green pepper, cut into 1-inch pieces*
2   *teaspoons fresh ginger (or 1/2 teaspoon powdered ginger)*
3/4 *cup toasted walnuts or cashews (toast in oven for approximately 5 minutes)*

Mix chicken broth, cornstarch, soy sauce, white wine and brown sugar in a bowl. Set aside.

In a wok or large frying pan, heat oil. Stir-fry chicken pieces over medium-high heat until chicken loses most of its pink color inside. Add onions, peppers and ginger to the wok. Stir well. Add 2 to 4 tablespoons of the chicken broth mixture. Cover quickly and cook for 3 minutes.

Uncover and add the remaining chicken broth mixture. Stir thoroughly over medium heat for 30 to 40 seconds.

Add nuts, stir lightly, and serve.

SERVES 4–6.

SMOTHERED CHICKEN

The Smothers Brothers love this. Ha Ha!

4	*skinless, boneless chicken breasts*
2	*teaspoons olive oil*
	pepper to taste
4	*garlic cloves, minced*
1	*onion, minced*
1/4	*teaspoon paprika*
2	*tablespoons flour*
1 1/2	*cups chicken broth*
1	*tablespoon soy sauce*
18–20	*mushrooms, sliced*
4	*cups cooked brown or white rice*
2	*teaspoons sesame seeds*

Set chicken in deep broiling pan. Season with olive oil, pepper, garlic, onion and paprika.

Set broiler approximately 5 inches from heat. Broil chicken 3 minutes on one side, turn and broil one minute on the other side. Remove and set aside.

In a mixing bowl, stir flour into broth and soy sauce until flour dissolves. Add mushrooms. Pour the broth mixture into a saucepan and cook over medium heat while stirring constantly until sauce thickens.

Slice and arrange the chicken breasts on rice, and smother everything with the mushroom sauce. Sprinkle with sesame seeds. Serve and stand back!

SERVES 4.

STIR-FRY CHICKEN

This is real quick, once you've got the vegetables chopped.

2   *tablespoons olive oil*
2   *tablespoons garlic, chopped*
2   *chicken breasts, cut into bite-size pieces*
1   *small onion, sliced*
4   *mushrooms, sliced*
1   *green pepper, sliced*
8   *asparagus, cut into pieces*
1   *tomato, coarsely chopped*
2   *stalks celery, chopped diagonally*
1/2 *teaspoon oregano*
    pepper to taste
4   *tablespoons white wine*
2   *cups cooked white or brown rice*
    juice of one lemon
4   *tablespoons sesame seeds*

In a hot wok or large frying pan, add olive oil and garlic. Sauté chicken breasts over high heat for about 2 minutes. Then add onion, mushrooms, green pepper, asparagus, tomato, celery, oregano and pepper to taste. Add white wine, then cover immediately. Cook for about 3 to 5 minutes until chicken is cooked through and vegetables are crisp.

Serve chicken and vegetables over rice. Sprinkle with lemon juice and sesame seeds and serve.

SERVES 2.

GOBBLE GOBBLE, GOOD GOOD, EASY EASY TURKEY

This mixture works well for meatballs, meat loaf, burgers and stuffing for red peppers.

2   *tablespoons olive oil*
2   *garlic cloves, minced*
1   *medium onion, minced*
1   *medium carrot, minced or grated*
2   *tablespoons fresh basil, minced*
8   *mushrooms, chopped*
1   *cup seasoned bread crumbs*
$^1/_2$ *cup grated nonfat cheese*
2   *eggs*
1   *pound ground turkey*
    pepper to taste

Pour oil in a large saucepan. Sauté garlic, onion, carrot, basil and mushrooms until translucent. Put in a large mixing bowl with bread crumbs, cheese, eggs, turkey and pepper. Mix thoroughly.

For meatballs: Using an ice-cream scoop, make meatballs. Arrange on a greased piece of aluminum foil in a baking pan and bake at 350 degrees for 30 minutes. Or brown in a frying pan with olive oil.

For meat loaf: Place in a greased loaf pan, top with 2 tablespoons ketchup, and bake for 1 hour at 375 degrees.

For patties: Shape into patties, and you're ready to broil or fry.

For stuffing vegetables: Stuff into parboiled green or red peppers, or into large mushroom caps. Bake at 350 degrees for 35 minutes.

SERVES 4.

SAUSAGES WITH PEPPERS AND ONIONS

I use turkey sausage, or if you like—pork!

1 tablespoon olive oil
2 garlic cloves, minced
1 pound sausage
1 red pepper, cut into finger wedges
1 green pepper, cut into finger wedges
1 onion, sliced into crescents

Pour oil in a large frying pan and sauté garlic for 30 seconds. Add sausage and cook uncovered for 20 minutes, turning once during that time.

Add the peppers and onion and cook for 10 minutes. Cover pan and cook for another 10 minutes.

Serve with bread and large salad and eat hearty.

SERVES 4.

This is me when Bing Crosby was so popular, hanging on to an unlit pipe.

TURKEY DARK MEAT (THIGHS AND LEGS) WITH VEGETABLES AND POTATOES

You can boast about this.

1   *tablespoon chopped fresh tarragon*
1/2 teaspoon freshly ground black pepper
4   *turkey thighs and legs, skin removed*
3   *large carrots, peeled and cut into large chunks*
3   *stalks celery, cut into large chunks*
2   *potatoes with skins, cut into quarters*
1   *large onion, peeled and cut into large chunks*
1   *leek, sliced vertically*
    juice of one lemon

Sprinkle tarragon and pepper over turkey parts. Place turkey in roasting pan surrounded by vegetables. Cover and bake at 350 degrees for 1¹/₂ hours.

Sprinkle turkey with lemon juice and serve with vegetables, potatoes and pan juice.

SERVES 6–8.

Slim Pickens about to cold-cock me in Mel Brooks's *Blazing Saddles.*

June Taylor

Me and the amazing June Taylor.

I worked with the talented June Taylor in *Around the World in Eighty Days* and on the "Jackie Gleason Show." June is a great friend of ours and I love her with all my heart. She's one of the bravest people I've ever met in my entire life. When we were doing the show at Jones Beach, there were sixty people in the cast. I had no idea how she was going to manipulate us around that stage. June sat crosslegged on a giant table with a megaphone, instructing us from a hundred feet away, saying things like, "Dom, you go near the camel"... "Robert Clary, you get into the balloon that's going to be airborne any minute"... "All the chorus girls in pink bows, get right in front of the elephant"... "David Atkinson, get out of the rickshaw and run for the balloon"... "All the chorus boys dressed as soldiers, enter from upstage right and chase him"... "And the people with green bows, come center and stay back because the ostrich will be running right in front of you"... "Send all the people in onstage left as soon as the boat lands and lets off the twelve policemen." And so it went. Nothing seemed to faze her.

Me and the great one!

I was impressed with June as she staged incredible numbers for Jackie Gleason. He looked great surrounded by June Taylor dancers. When Jackie Gleason invited me to perform in the Dom DeLuise show in Florida, it was June who staged the numbers for me with such ease that I was able to look at the whole production number and as June suggested, just watch the guy with the blue sweater. "He's doing what you should do." I watched the number, then we would do it again, and it was a snap for me, and it always looked fantastic. Marilyn, Jackie Gleason's widow, has often been seen with June, and they are enthusiastic and zestful, and a great deal of fun to be with. They both seem to have "joie de vivre," I guess because they're sisters.

Through the years Carol and I have been very close to June, and she has enhanced our lives tenfold. She recently had a giant charity show called "Showoffs" and I had the privilege of working with her and her very talented cast, and she put on a show that was absolutely marvelous. I think I have learned an enormous lesson from my sweet, amazing friend. Someone gives her a job to do, saying, "I know it's impossible." June says, "It is impossible and it can't be done." And then she rubs her hands together, smiles a little devilish smile, and says with her heart full of courage, "Let's get started." And with her talented visions, I'll be damned if she doesn't lead us all to the top of the mountain, where, with her feet planted firmly on the uppermost ridge, she sees the beautiful view of happy accomplishment, raises her banner yet closer to the sky, and says, "Well, gang, we did it."

Thanks for the impossible. You did it, June! Go catch a star.

DOM'S GROUND TURKEY BURGERS

1¹/₂ *pounds ground turkey*
1   *medium onion, minced*
2   *eggs (or equivalent)*
1   *teaspoon thyme*
1   *teaspoon chopped parsley*
     pepper to taste
     olive-oil spray

In a large mixing bowl, add all ingredients except olive oil. Mix thoroughly. Shape into patties.

Spray oil in a Teflon pan. Fry patties for about 3 minutes on each side until pink is gone from the center and patties are firm.

SERVES 4.

DOM'S GOBBLE GOBBLE

1 *teaspoon mustard*
3 *teaspoons olive oil*
1 *teaspoon thyme*
2 *teaspoons rosemary*
1 *pound of turkey breast cutlets, about ¹/₂ inch thick*
  (or use chicken breasts)

Combine mustard, oil and herbs in a bowl.

In a greased baking dish place the turkey cutlets (or chicken breasts) and coat with mustard mixture.

Place in a preheated 350-degree oven for 10 minutes or until the pink is just gone, or under the broiler for about 4 minutes or until the pink is gone.

Serve with a cold salad and some hot bread.

SERVES 5.

TURKEY STUFFED VEGETABLES

zucchini
red peppers
large mushrooms
tomatoes
Ground Turkey (see page 103)
marinara sauce

Zucchini: Cut zucchini lengthwise and scoop out middle with a spoon. Fill with basic ground turkey mixture.

Peppers: Cut peppers lengthwise and remove stems and seeds. Parboil for 3 minutes. Fill with basic ground turkey mixture.

Mushrooms: Wash mushrooms thoroughly. Remove stems. Fill caps with basic ground turkey mixture.

Tomatoes: Cut tomato in half and remove soft center. Fill hollow with basic ground turkey mixture.

Arrange vegetables in the bottom of a baking dish. Top with marinara sauce and cover. Bake at 350 degrees for 1 hour.

Serve with mashed potatoes, broccoli and salad.

SERVES 4.

Meat

MEATBALLS, MEAT LOAF OR BURGERS

This was originally my mamma's meatball recipe. Thank you, Mamma.

Any shape that suits you!

3   *pounds ground turkey, beef, veal, pork or any combination*
    (I like turkey)
1   *onion, finely chopped*
5   *garlic cloves, minced*
5   *eggs*
2   *cups milk*
2   *cups seasoned bread crumbs*
    pepper to taste
3/4 *cup grated cheese*
1   *cup fresh parsley, chopped*
1/2 *cup pignoli (pine nuts) (optional)*

Mix all ingredients in a large bowl.

Meatballs: Keep putting an ice-cream scooper back into a cup of hot water as you make the meatballs. (They will come out of the scooper easier.) Arrange meatballs on a lightly greased piece of aluminum foil in a baking pan. Bake at 350 degrees for 20 minutes or brown in a little olive oil in a Teflon pan. Cool them and put them in Ziploc bags. They freeze great.

Meat loaf: Place in a greased loaf pan, coat top with ketchup, and bake at 350 degrees for 1 hour.

Burgers: Shape into patties and you're ready to bake, broil or fry.

MAKES ABOUT 80 MEATBALLS, ABOUT 4 OR 5 MEAT LOAVES, ABOUT 25 BURGERS.

CHUCK ROAST WITH VEGETABLES

I love Chuck. I went to school with him.

6   *pounds boneless beef chuck*
    pepper to taste
1/2 *cup flour*
2   *tablespoons olive oil*
2   *cups beef bouillon*
6   *potatoes, peeled and cut in half*
12 *small onions, peeled*
3   *medium white turnips, peeled and cut in half (optional)*
12 *small carrots, peeled*
1   *teaspoon flour*

A big pussy cat and me.

Season meat with pepper. Thoroughly coat meat with flour. In an iron skillet, brown meat well in 2 tablespoons olive oil.

Transfer meat to a roasting pan. Add 1 cup bouillon and cover. Roast at 350 degrees for 1 hour, basting occasionally. Remove roast from oven, and position all vegetables around the roast. Pour the remaining cup of bouillon over them. Cover and return to oven, lowered to 275 degrees, for another hour, or until tender. Transfer to platter and let sit for 15 minutes.

While keeping vegetables warm, remove string from meat, slice on cutting board, and arrange on serving platter. Arrange vegetables around meat.

For gravy: In a small saucepan, heat about 1/2 cup of the juice from the pan over low flame (discard the fat). Mix 1 teaspoon flour with 1/2 cup water. Add flour and water mixture slowly to juice to prevent lumps. Stir until thickened, and serve with the roast.

SERVES 8–10.

Tom Hennen

I was in Westbury, Long Island, with Jerry Vale, and we had sold-out houses. They were so sold-out that my wife had to sit in a folding chair. I was staying in a hotel and when I went for a newspaper I found myself face-to-face with Tom Hennen, the astronaut. I was just reading about him in the newspaper, and he wanted my autograph and I wanted his autograph. He was giving a lecture about what it was like to be in orbit. We sat down for coffee and two and a half hours later we were talking about things like how fast that thing goes around the earth. Tom told me to blink and he said, "You have just traveled six miles." I asked him, "How long does it take to orbit around the earth one time?" And he said, "Guess," and I said I thought it would take about a day and a half, which I thought was pretty fast. He corrected me and told me it was an hour and a half. He said in one day he would go around the earth eleven times. He said that he could look out the window and see the entire earth. He said that as he passed over continents, he got used to the configurations, and could tell at a glance which was which continent.

Tom was like a kid as he shared some of his amazing information with me, which the kid in me received gratefully. He said there were fourteen astronauts, men and women, confined to a room that was 8 by 8 feet. I said, "Did you feel claustrophobic?" He said no, because they were able to use the floor and the walls and the ceiling with equal efficiency. If they were sleeping there would be some people on the floor,

some on the walls, and some on the ceiling. There really wasn't an up or down. If you wanted to sleep on the ceiling you attached yourself to Velcro, and as you slept you could look across and see somebody sleeping on the opposite floor or ceiling if you knew which way was up. He said all the flat surfaces had little pieces of Velcro and if you were writing a letter you could keep track of your pen by attaching it to a piece of Velcro.

He talked about drinking orange juice from a container with a straw. He said when he sipped orange juice from the container, the entire contents of the orange juice came out of the container and floated in front of him in a ball. The cabin was pressurized but there was no gravity. Tom said if you carefully took the straw and inserted it in the center of the floating orange juice, you could sip it all down, in essence drinking from the air. I can't imagine what it would be like to eat a portion of spaghetti and meatballs that was airborne. If you sprinkled grated cheese on your pasta there is no telling where the cheese would end up. It all sounds very bizarre. If you were having a hot dog, bun, sauerkraut and mustard, you could take a few bites and finish it off with a lick of mustard, hands not coming into play at all.

He said if two people stand together and gently push each other with the index finger, they would go across the room. He said they were together a long time, and that they all circled the earth about ninety-two times. Tom shared with me the intricate manner in which they had to go to the bathroom. I have come to the conclusion that to be an astronaut is also to be a good sport.

This incredibly generous man is working with Make A Wish Foundation, which grants the wishes of children who are ill. He was devoting a giant amount of his energy to the foundation, and it seemed to me with all his heart.

We had an opportunity to talk to his mother on the phone and she was adorable. I got to call her again to check on her address so I could send her EAT THIS. We went to lunch and shared some pasta and some laughs. When I put the grated cheese on my spaghetti it fell directly on the pasta. Will wonders never cease? Thank you, Tom.

NORMA'S LIKE YOU NEVER TASTED IT BEFORE...SWEET 'N' SOUR BEEF

My friend Michael invited me to a seder at his mom and dad's house. It was glorious. His parents, Cantor Alan Edwards and his wife, Norma, who is a nurse, served something that was so delicious and so different for me! I not only took some home to enjoy the next day, I also begged for the recipe! Now my hostess happened to talk very fast. Norma is a very peppy broad! I was hysterical from laughing but I got it all down, and she only had to say it twice.

So for something different, read on. Norma told me that she used to brown the beef and do lots of other steps but she said it comes out the same either way. Just throw it all in the pot, cover it, and go play with your grandkids (in her case it's Sarah Rose and Rachael).

If you are adventurous and care to take a risk that will pay off in a very unique dish and compliments, try her Sweet 'n' Sour Beef.

Michael helped me write out the recipe and when I looked at it I said, "Wait, there is wine in this recipe your mother didn't mention." When I said when does the wine go in, Michael said, "As soon as my mother leaves the kitchen." So the answer is when you leave the kitchen tell your husband to add $1/2$ glass of wine! That's the way they do it!

6–8 *pounds beef*
2   *large onions, sliced into crescents*
4–6 *garlic cloves, stuck in the beef*
1   *cup stock*
4   *tablespoons lemon juice or vinegar*
4   *tablespoons ketchup*
$1/2$ *cup raisins*
4   *tablespoons brown sugar*
$1/2$ *cup sweet grape wine, such as Maneschewitz*

Cook in preheated oven at 350 degrees for approximately 2 hours.

Here's all my friend told me to do: Get a large roasting pan and put some onion at the bottom, add your beef, and sprinkle all the other stuff on top of and around it, then cover and cook till the cows come home.

SERVES 10–15.

DOM'S MAMMA'S VEAL OR PORK OR CHICKEN OR TURKEY CUTLETS

My son Peter throws these babies in the air! They never hit the ground!

1	*pound veal, pork, chicken or turkey cutlets, sliced very thin and pounded flat between 2 pieces of waxed paper*
1	*cup flavored bread crumbs*
3 or 4	*large eggs*
	olive oil

First bread the pounded cutlets with the crumbs and set aside. In a mixing bowl, place the eggs and beat very well. Dip breaded cutlets in egg mixture one by one, return to crumbs and recoat cutlets.

Heat 4 tablespoons of oil in a frying pan to medium-hot. Fry the cutlets until golden brown on both sides. Remove from pan and place on paper towels to absorb excess oil. Use more oil as needed. Serve plain with lemon wedges.

SERVES 4–5.

VARIATION: Top each pork, chicken or turkey cutlet with tomato sauce and shredded mozzarella cheese and bake in 300-degree oven for 20 minutes.

VEAL ROAST WITH ROSEMARY

I love this veal roast—it's so European.

1   *3- to 4-pound veal rump roast*
    freshly ground black pepper
2   *tablespoons oil*
1/2 *cup water*
1/2 *cup white wine*
4   *garlic cloves, chopped*
1   *teaspoon rosemary*
3   *medium onions, sliced into*
    crescents
3   *carrots, halved*

Sprinkle roast with pepper to taste. In heavy kettle or roasting pan, heat oil. Add meat and brown all over. Place a rack under the meat, add water, wine, garlic and rosemary. Cover and roast in oven at 350 degrees for 2 hours. A half hour before meat is ready, add onions and carrots.

Transfer meat and vegetables to hot platter. Slice thin and serve.

Great with mashed or sweet potatoes and broccoli. And of course a salad!

SERVES 6.

VEAL WITH WHITE WINE AND MUSHROOMS

The smell alone satisfies.

2	3-pound pieces bottom round veal
	pepper to taste
1 1/2	cups white wine
1	bay leaf
3	garlic cloves, slivered
1	teaspoon rosemary
1/2	teaspoon tarragon
1/4	cup white wine
1	tablespoon flour
2	pounds mushrooms, quartered

Set meat in large roasting pan. Pepper to taste. Add 1 1/2 cups wine, bay leaf, garlic, rosemary and tarragon. Roast at 350 degrees for 1 hour and 20 minutes, basting two or three times.

Remove meat from oven and drain off 2 or 3 cups of liquid. If there is not enough liquid, add white wine. Skim off fat.

Place meat juice in a large saucepan. Mix 1/4 cup wine and flour together until smooth. Add to meat juice. Heat slowly while stirring constantly. Stir in mushrooms and cook for 3 minutes.

Place veal on serving platter and cut vertically into 1/3-inch-thick slices. Drizzle with sauce.

SERVES 8–10.

DOM'S VEAL OR CHICKEN OR TURKEY OR PORK PICCATA

1 *pound thinly cut veal scaloppine (or chicken, turkey or pork)*
3 *tablespoons flour*
4 *tablespoons butter*
1/2 *pound fresh mushrooms, sliced*
1/2 *lemon*
1/2 *cup dry white wine*
  fresh parsley sprigs
  lemon slices

Cut veal (chicken, turkey or pork) into serving pieces then coat each piece with flour. Heat butter in a skillet until it sizzles. Add meat and cook over medium-high heat until lightly browned on both sides. Add sliced mushrooms and sauté until brown. Squeeze lemon over veal (or whatever) in pan, then add wine, swoosh everything around in pan, and cook 1 minute more.

Arrange on serving platter, garnish with parsley sprigs and lemon slices.

Serve linguine with oil and garlic with this type of veal.

SERVES 4.

Shari Lewis and Lamb Chop

1960

1997

Two photos of Shari and Lamb Chop taken about thirty years apart. I didn't know lamb lasted that long.

*T*he very first time I was on television, I was doing a character called Kenny Katchum. I was very excited because I was going to have the opportunity to work with Shari Lewis and Lamb Chop. Shari is a brilliant ventriloquist. She can make Lamb Chop and Charlie Horse talk and sing and emote in any way. You will never see her lips move. Never! Even though you know she is doing the voices for all her characters, there is no way that even occurs to you while you watch the scene because you are completely involved emotionally and you only focus on what is going to happen next, not on whose lips are moving. Edgar Bergen, another brilliant ventriloquist who happens to be the father of Candice Bergen (Murphy Brown, who had a baby out of wedlock, to which the vice president of America objected strongly) moved his lips while Charlie McCarthy was talking. I remember when I was a kid I used to say I loved Charlie McCarthy but I didn't particularly care for Edgar Bergen. Remember, he was really brilliant. The infamous Mae West flirted with Charlie McCarthy in a movie once: "Even though you're a dummy, why don't you come up and see me sometime? I'll let you play with my woodpile." Edgar Bergen's career spanned many years; he became an excellent character actor in his later years. He was wonderful in the movie *I Remember Mama* as the gentle suitor.

I have worked with Shari periodically through the years. I always felt a kindred spirit with all of her characters, and my wife and I are crazy about Shari and her wonderful husband, Jeremy Tarcher, who is a publisher and one of the most gentle, funny and brilliant men you'd ever want to meet.

But recently in Canada, the grown-up me had the thrilling experience of being a guest on Shari's new Emmy award–winning show that seemed to get the approval of a lot of sophisticated people. It was called "Shari's Seder Special." Alan Thicke from Canada and Robert Guillaume, along with me, had a chance to examine with care, love and humor the intricacies of the many parts involved in a seder. So we had soup, salad, matzo, vegetables, potatoes and, pardon the expression lamb! Here's a toast to Shari Lewis and her amazing energy, beauty and her seemingly brave ability to enjoy lamb.

Out of the four of us, me, Shari, Lamb Chop and Charlie Horse, I am the only one who unfortunately seems to have visibly, showed the aging process. If it's possible, I think Shari looks better than she ever has. It's from all that lamb!

TURKISH SHISH KABOB

Wear a turban if you want—it's terrific!

2–3 *pounds boned leg of lamb, cut into 1½-inch cubes (also works with veal, beef, pork, turkey, chicken or sausage)*
1 *medium onion, minced pepper to taste*
1½ *teaspoons dried oregano*
6 *tablespoons olive oil*
1 *medium onion, cut into quarters*
6–8 *tomatoes, not too ripe, in large wedges*
12 *medium mushrooms, whole*
2 *green peppers, cut into 2-inch chunks*
2 *red peppers, cut into 2-inch chunks pilaf or rice lemon wedges*

Light the grill 1 hour before cooking.

A couple of hours before, put lamb in a large bowl. Add minced onion, pepper, oregano and oil and mix well. Cover and refrigerate.

Before cooking, on metal skewers, alternate lamb cubes, onions, tomatoes, mushrooms and peppers, leaving ¼ inch between each piece.

Brush vegetables lightly with oil, then grill 5 inches above hot coals for 10 to 15 minutes, just until center of lamb is still a little pink. Turn frequently. Brush all pieces with enough oil to keep moist while cooking.

Using fork, push shish kabob off skewer onto a serving plate. Serve over pilaf. Garnish with lemon wedges.

SERVES 8.

OPTIONAL: If making in the broiler, preheat 10 minutes, broil about 4 inches away for about 10 to 12 minutes, turning once, brushing with oil before.

You are in charge. If you want your lamb rare, medium or well—Enjoy!

Michael Chiklis

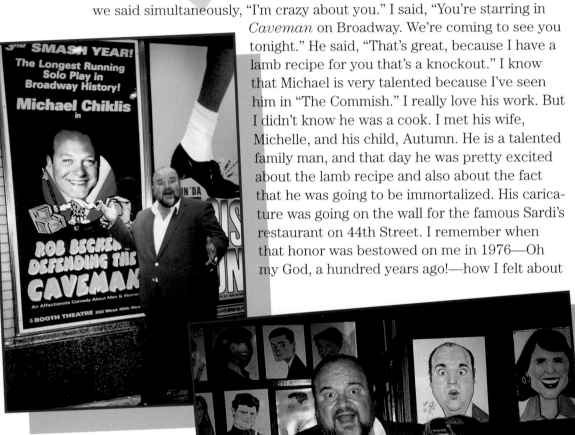

Carol and I were in New York and we were walking through Shubert Alley and I came face-to-face with Michael Chiklis. "Oh," we said simultaneously, "I'm crazy about you." I said, "You're starring in *Caveman* on Broadway. We're coming to see you tonight." He said, "That's great, because I have a lamb recipe for you that's a knockout." I know that Michael is very talented because I've seen him in "The Commish." I really love his work. But I didn't know he was a cook. I met his wife, Michelle, and his child, Autumn. He is a talented family man, and that day he was pretty excited about the lamb recipe and also about the fact that he was going to be immortalized. His caricature was going on the wall for the famous Sardi's restaurant on 44th Street. I remember when that honor was bestowed on me in 1976—Oh my God, a hundred years ago!—how I felt about it, and it was no small thing. I was thrilled! I congratulated Michael. By the way, he was hysterically funny in *Caveman,* took my lamb recipe, got Carol, and disappeared for lunch at Sardi's with our good friend Bruce Laffey. By the way, we sat directly under my caricature. Oh, joy!

DOM'S FRIEND MICHAEL CHIKLIS' LAMB ROAST

1	leg of lamb, glands removed
8–10	garlic cloves, peeled
8–10	potatoes, peeled and halved
6–8	carrots, peeled and quartered
4	onions, sliced into crescents
	juice of 2 lemons—and then throw the lemon skins in the roasting pan
1/2	cup light Karo syrup
1	tablespoon rosemary
1	tablespoon oregano
1	tablespoon parsley
	pepper to taste
6	shallots, minced
1	cup red or white wine

Make a slit for each clove of garlic and insert into the meat.

Place lamb in large roasting pan. Surround lamb with potatoes, carrots and onions. If not enough room, put lamb on top of vegetables. Coat outside of lamb with Karo syrup. It seals in the flavors and keeps it moist and holds spices in place. Sprinkle with rosemary, oregano, parsley and pepper, then top off with minced shallots. Pour wine in the bottom of roasting pan. Place in a 350-degree oven for 1½ hours. Uncover and cook an additional ½ hour.

Michael tells me that this is great with a big Greek salad and he likes al dente steamed asparagus on the side. It sounds as delicious as Michael's acting.

You never know who you're going to meet in Shubert Alley!

IF LEG OF LAMB IS FOUR POUNDS, YOU CAN FIGURE IT SERVES 10 TO 12 PEOPLE (ABOUT THREE PORTIONS PER POUND).

VEAL, CHICKEN OR BEEF CACCIATORE

This dish is even better the next day.

2   *pounds veal, cut into 2-inch cubes*
2   *tablespoons olive oil*
2   *large ripe tomatoes, cut into sixths*
2   *tablespoons Worcestershire sauce*
2   *stalks celery, cut up*
1   *green pepper, sliced thick*
1   *red pepper, sliced thick*
1   *cup white wine*
½   *teaspoon rosemary*
1   *teaspoon oregano*
2   *small onions, diced*
      pepper to taste
½   *cup Italian parsley, chopped*
10   *mushrooms, quartered*

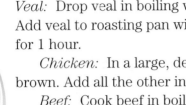

Veal: Drop veal in boiling water for 10 minutes. Drain, discard water. Add veal to roasting pan with all other ingredients and cook medium-low for 1 hour.

Chicken: In a large, deep skillet, brown chicken in oil until golden brown. Add all the other ingredients. Cover and simmer for 1 hour.

Beef: Cook beef in boiling water for one hour. Drain, discard water. Add beef to roasting pan with all the rest of the ingredients and cook 1 hour longer.

Serve with noodles or rice.

Serves 4–6

VEAL SCALOPPINE

Very simple and it's great to boot!

1	*pound veal cutlets*
	flour
6	*tablespoons olive oil*
1	*garlic clove, minced*
	pepper to taste
1/2	*cup sherry*
2	*tablespoons chopped parsley*
8–12	*mushrooms, sliced*

Slice veal and place between two pieces of wax paper. Pound thin with a mallet to about 1/4 inch. Cover with flour.

Add oil to a large skillet. Sauté veal and garlic for 3 to 4 minutes on each side. Sprinkle veal with pepper. Add sherry, parsley and mushrooms. Simmer 10 minutes.

Serve with anything. Try potatoes, rice, pasta, broccoli or sliced, baked sweet potatoes.

Serves 4.

DOM'S ROASTED COUNTRY-STYLE RABBIT

1/2 cup flour
     black pepper
1/4 teaspoon cayenne pepper
1   rabbit, cut into 8 pieces
4   garlic cloves, minced
4   tablespoons olive oil
1/2 cup dry white wine or beer
1   teaspoon flour
1   cup chicken broth
6   mushrooms, sliced

Combine flour and pepper in a paper or plastic bag. Place rabbit in bag and shake to coat. Then in a Teflon pan brown rabbit and garlic in oil. Place pieces in a roasting pan. Add wine or beer to bottom of pan and bake uncovered at 375 degrees for 1 hour.

Remove rabbit to a heated platter. Mix flour and chicken broth and sliced mushrooms, add to pan drippings and stir over low heat for about 4 minutes.

SERVE THIS GRAVY WITH:
mashed potatoes
mushrooms
rice
noodles or
green vegetable.

Remember: This also works with chicken.

SERVES 4.

Michael and Mr. Bunny.

DOM'S RABBIT OR CHICKEN FRICASSEE

1/2	cup flour
	pepper
2	rabbits, each cut into 8 pieces
2	tablespoons olive oil
2	cups chicken broth
2	sprigs parsley, chopped
1/2	teaspoon dried marjoram
1/2	teaspoon dried oregano
1/4	teaspoon ground allspice
1/4	teaspoon ground cloves
1/2	cup lemon juice
1	small onion, minced
10–12	mushrooms, sliced
1	tablespoon flour

Place flour in a paper bag or plastic bag and season to taste with pepper. Shake rabbit pieces in bag to coat with flour.

In a Teflon pan brown rabbit pieces on both sides in oil. Reduce heat, add 1 cup of chicken broth, parsley, marjoram, oregano, allspice, cloves and lemon juice. Cover and simmer over low heat for 50 minutes. Add minced onion and mushrooms and simmer for 10 minutes more. Remove rabbit to a warm platter.

Blend remaining cup of chicken broth with 1 tablespoon of flour and add to pan drippings. Cook over medium-low heat about 2 1/2 minutes, stirring until gravy is thickened.

Pour some gravy over rabbit and serve remainder on side.

SERVE WITH:
barley pilaf
peas and onions
twice-baked potatoes
acorn squash
carrots.

Remember: This also works fantastically with chicken.

SERVES 6–8.

Dean Martin—The Gift!

I was on "Dean Martin's Summer Show" for a long time—twelve years. I started out with Dan Rowan and Dick Martin who later became famous for "Laugh In" with Ruth Buzzi, Goldie Hawn and Lily Tomlin. Dean was spectacular, spontaneous, stupendous, sexy and he sang good. I think that everyone who was watching the show came to the conclusion that Dean was having a ball, and he was. The man responsible for this phenomenon was Greg Garrison who was originally the director of the show and who quickly realized that Dean really needed to be completely free to be able to go in any direction and be able to say anything he wanted while he was reading the cue cards. Greg set it up so that Dean could come in one day, watch the show being performed with his stand-in, and as soon as the

Dean was so much fun. Often he would slip off the barber chair, laughing!

audience arrived he would perform the show once. That was the key feeling about it—it looked like it was spontaneous, it smelled alive.

Before I worked with Dean himself, I was on the "Dean Martin Summer Show" and Dean wasn't on it. I guess Greg Garrison thought I was good enough to appear on the "Dean Martin Show." I was young and scared. When I performed, my mouth was so dry I couldn't lick my lips if you paid me. The audience was aware of how nervous I

My son Peter got more laughs than Dean in the sketch!

was. Greg took me to Dean's room and said, "I want Dom to try the routine again." Dean got off the couch, gave me a hug, kissed my cheek, made a few jokes and pinched my ass as I left the room. He relaxed me! His sweetness and his caring and his indulgence in whatever I was going through came from a very dear and kind man, because the second time we did it, the routine went well, and the audience laughed. Dean laughed and gave me support, and he didn't have to do that. As I write this I'm very touched because I feel embraced by him even now that Dean is gone. Toward the end of the twelve years I was doing every single show as Dean's barber. Dean would sit in the chair and read the cards, I would trim his hair, and people would come in and get their hair trimmed by Nipsey Russell—people like Jack Benny, Jimmy Stewart, Buddy Hackett, Don Rickles and Peter Sellers, who in the middle of one routine, decided to change his character and became very effeminate. I had to use all my strength to keep Dean in the barber chair. He kept slipping off the seat, he was laughing so much. My life has been so enriched because of Dean Martin! I miss him, but to have worked with him—oh, what a gift. Thank you, God.

DOM'S RABBIT DIJON (ROASTED)

1   *rabbit, cut into 8 pieces*
1   *8-oz. jar Dijon mustard*
4   *tablespoons olive oil*
4   *garlic cloves, minced*
2   *teaspoons flour*
1/2 *cup chicken broth*
1/4 *cup cognac*
1   *tablespoon lemon juice*

Spread rabbit pieces liberally with mustard and oil on both sides. Store in refrigerator for several hours

Place pieces in a casserole, add garlic and roast uncovered at 350 degrees for 1 hour. Remove rabbit to a hot platter and keep warm. Blend flour with broth and add to pan drippings. Stir till smooth and thickened; do not boil.

Add cognac and 1 tablespoon lemon juice. Stir for about 4 minutes over medium heat. Pour over rabbit pieces.

SERVE WITH YOUR CHOICE OF:
mashed potatoes
glazed carrots
sautéed mushrooms
broccoli
wild and brown rice
corn
parsnips.

Chicken loves "Dijon" too!

SERVES 4.

DOM'S PHEASANT IN WINE

Remember chickens love wine!

1   *whole pheasant*
2   *stalks celery*
1   *onion, diced*
2   *scallions*
2   *garlic cloves, chopped*
1   *tart apple, chopped*
2   *tablespoons olive oil*
1/4 cup brandy
1/2 cup chicken stock
1   *cup white wine*
1   *cup nonfat sour cream*
1/2 cup walnuts
    parsley sprigs

Stuff pheasant with celery, onion, scallions, garlic and apple. Brown bird in pan on all sides in oil. Pour warmed brandy over pheasant, ignite. When flame is out, place bird in casserole. Add chicken stock and wine to pan and simmer, stirring to get any pan drippings. Pour sauce over pheasant, cover, and bake at 350 degrees for 45 minutes.

Just before serving, stir sour cream into pan juices and season with pepper.

Garnish with walnuts and parsley.

SERVES 2 OR 3, OR 1 HUNGRY HUSBAND, FRIEND OR LOVER.

DOM'S CHRISTMAS GOOSE

1   *14- to 16-pound goose*
1   *teaspoon black pepper*
1   *onion, chopped*
2   *teaspoons dry mustard*
1   *teaspoon ginger*
1/4 *teaspoon mace*
2   *teaspoons herb seasoning*
1   *cup red wine*
1   *tablespoon vegetable flakes*
6   *cloves*
2   *teaspoons allspice*
2   *teaspoons cardamom*
2   *cups chicken broth*
2   *tablespoons flour*
     fruit
     parsley
     orange marmalade

Rinse goose inside and out. Let Tiny Tim pat dry!

Combine pepper, onion, dry mustard, ginger, mace and herb seasoning. Rub these seasonings inside the cavity and on the outside of goose. Using a fine sharp fork, pierce the goose skin all over. This allows the excess fat to cook out.

Place goose on a rack in a roasting pan. Roast in a 450-degree oven for about 30 minutes. Remove fat. Reduce heat to 325 degrees and continue to roast, allowing 30 minutes per pound. Baste several times with red wine. After about an hour, add vegetable flakes, allspice, cardamom, push cloves into skin, and continue cooking.

When goose is done, remove to a heated platter. Pour off fat leaving the browned bits in the roasting pan. Mix chicken broth and flour and add to pan drippings, stirring over low heat for about 4 minutes until gravy is thickened.

Serve goose on hot platter with attractive arrangement of fruit and garnish with parsley. Serve with orange marmalade on the side.

Our Christmas family!
How lucky can I get!

Oh and don't forget to ask Tiny Tim to help set the table.

SERVE WITH:
baked potatoes
separately baked stuffing
brown rice
parsnips
cranberry sauce
sweet potatoes
stuffed mushrooms
and Tiny Tim, of course.

God Bless us every one!

SERVES 15–20.

My Christmas Lesson

There was a Christmas where I was overworked and overwhelmed, and as much as I like Christmas, I was over-Christmased. I was involved in a television show and I was at Tiffany's (the jewelry store) buying three hundred and fifty little gifts for the cast and crew when a robbery took place where three people had guns and were smashing glass counters and shouting obscenities. Shots were fired, and in the middle of the robbery the security guard raised his hands and shouted, "Halt!" and he was shot and fell down to the floor. We were all so scared. We were told to lie facedown on the floor, and it was all very scary. I thought I was going to die with my face two inches from the rug, and I thought, "I should have gone to Macy's."

My friend, Laura Van Mannen, who worked at Tiffany's, was pregnant and was lying on the floor next to me, with our faces almost touching. Not surprisingly, she was pretty terrified, and so was I—Big time! By the time the men left, we were all trembling in our boots. It was probably the longest three and a half minutes of my life. After the robbers left, I used my jacket to make a pillow for the guard, who was lying on the floor, sweating profusely. He was *obviously* in a state of shock. I undid his shirt, and the bullet hole was not bloody at all; it was just like a small hole. I stroked his head and I told him that help was on the way. I went around trying to comfort some of the other people. When I heard that NBC News wanted to tape my impression of the robbery, I was a basket case. I reluctantly did the interview.

Later that night as I opened the front door of my home, Peter had one of those toy machine guns that you crank and fire. It made a loud machine gun noise, and I almost went through the ceiling. I must have been pretty upset because I wept. Later that night when everything was pretty relaxed, my middle son, Michael, came into my arms and leaned on my chest. He said very sweetly, "Dad, what do you want for Christmas?" I said, without thinking, "Happiness, and you can't give it to me." I didn't regret it because I was thinking that the world was a pretty awful place, and to tell you the truth, after that, I didn't think too much more about it.

A couple of weeks later when we were giving out our gifts on Christmas morning, Michael came up to me in the midst of the distribution with a very light package, which I casually opened. My son had written on a piece of cardboard, with red crayon, the word "Happiness." Michael smiled and said very sweetly, "See, Dad, I did give you happiness!" The next couple of seconds I was gasping for air, and then I just wept. Michael's gift was simple, loving, and oh so disarming! Michael knew that I was happy because he could see that I was crying tears of joy. I hugged him and I could hear myself saying that it was the best Christmas present I had ever gotten. And indeed it was!

Fish

SHRIMP AND SCALLOP STIR-FRY

Al dente and well, it really tastes swell.

3	*tablespoons olive oil*
4	*garlic cloves, minced*
1	*onion, sliced into crescents*
6	*mushrooms, sliced*
2	*carrots, thinly sliced*
2	*stalks celery, diagonally sliced*
1	*medium tomato, chopped*
1/2	*pound shrimp, peeled, cleaned and deveined*
1/2	*pound scallops*
1/2	*cup white wine*
1	*tablespoon oyster sauce*
1	*tablespoon soy sauce*
1	*10-oz. can cream of mushroom soup (optional)*

Heat olive oil in a wok or large frying pan over high heat. Add garlic, onion, mushrooms, carrots, celery, tomato, shrimp and scallops, and stir-fry for 2 minutes.

Add white wine, oyster sauce and soy sauce. Cover and simmer for approximately 4 minutes.

Serve with rice or pasta.

SERVES 4–6.

OPTIONAL: For a creamier sauce, add 1 can cream of mushroom soup (undiluted) when adding wine.

Peter, me, a friend, our niece Regina, Burt, Carol, David and Michael during the filming of *The End*.

BROILED SHRIMP AND SCALLOPS

A treat for anyone.

1	*pound scallops*
1	*pound shrimp, peeled, cleaned and deveined*
4–6	*tablespoons olive oil*
4	*tablespoons fresh basil, chopped*
1/2	*teaspoon pepper*
4	*garlic cloves, minced*
	lemon wedges

Place shrimp and scallops in a broiling pan. Sprinkle with olive oil, fresh basil and pepper and put a dab of garlic on each piece.

Broil for 1^1/$_2$ minutes, then flip shrimp and scallops over and broil for an additional 1^1/$_2$ minutes.

Remove from broiler, arrange on serving plates and serve with lemon wedges.

SERVES 4–6.

CRABMEAT CASSEROLE

Good! Good! Good!

1/4 *pound lowfat margarine*
2   *tablespoons flour*
1   *pint light cream or nonfat sour cream*
1/2 *cup dry sherry*
     pepper to taste
1   *pound fresh or frozen king crabmeat*
1/2 *pound nonfat Swiss or Monterey Jack cheese, grated*
1   *onion, chopped*
1/2 *cup minced parsley*
2   *cups cooked rice*
6   *deviled eggs*
     lemon wedges

In a large frying pan, mix margarine and flour. Sauté over low heat and allow to bubble. Pour in cream or nonfat sour cream and sherry.

Add pepper to taste, then add crabmeat, Swiss cheese, onion and parsley. Set rice in the bottom of a medium casserole dish, and pour crabmeat mixture over the rice. Bake at 350 degrees approximately 1/2 hour until bubbly.

Garnish with deviled eggs and lemon wedges, and serve.

Oh, once your people taste this treat, there will be no crabs around!

SERVES 6–8.

FILLET OF SOLE WITH MUSHROOM SAUCE

Easy to eat anytime.

1   *15-oz. package frozen chopped spinach, thawed, or a pound of*
    fresh spinach (parboiled), chopped
8   *mushrooms, sliced*
1   *cup shredded lowfat Swiss cheese*
2   *pounds fillet of sole or flounder*
1   *8-oz. can cream of mushroom soup*
1/4 *teaspoon black pepper*
1/2 *cup sherry*
1/4 *teaspoon nutmeg*

Spread a large tablespoon of spinach, a few slices of mushrooms and
cheese over each fillet. Roll fillet up. Place fish rolls in a baking dish, seam
side down. Mix cream of mushroom soup, pepper, sherry and nutmeg, and
pour over fish rolls.

Bake at 350 degrees for approximately 35 to 40 minutes uncovered.

SERVES 4–6.

OPTIONAL: Substitute cooked chopped broccoli for chopped spinach.

Mom, a fish
that has seen
better days,
and me!

Me and Jeremy the Crow from The Secret of NIMH

I've been blessed with the opportunity to be the voice of many characters in animated films. I had a sweet beginning working with a wonderful man named Don Bluth when he did *The Secret of NIMH*. I was the voice of Jeremy the Crow, and I really cherish all those wonderful sessions when Jeremy the Crow and I got together. Since then I have done *An American Tail, Fievel Goes West, Oliver and Company, All Dogs Go to Heaven* (parts one and two) and the TV series. With *Dogs*, part one, I worked with my dear friend Burt Reynolds, and with *Dogs*, part two, with the wonderfully talented Charlie Sheen. For three and a half years I've been working with Steven Weber of "Wings" fame, one of the most talented men I know. He is so much fun that I run to work with him. He's done some amazing dramatic work and scared the pants off of me and Carol when he did *The Shining.* "Scaaaaree." But, oh, it's very comforting to know that my voice is "going to the dogs and cats and birds."

PAN-FRIED CATFISH

Well bless my catfish! Orange Roughy will taste as sweet.

1   *pound catfish fillets*
    pepper to taste
1/2 *cup lemon juice*
1/2 *cup seasoned bread crumbs*
4   *tablespoons grated nonfat cheese*
2   *tablespoons olive oil*
1   *lemon cut in wedges*
    parsley sprigs

Rinse fillets (do not dry) and sprinkle with pepper.

Combine bread crumbs and grated cheese in a shallow dish. Put lemon juice in another shallow dish. Drop fillets in lemon juice, and then in the bread crumb and cheese mixture to coat.

Heat oil in a frying pan over medium heat. Lay fish in pan and cook 2 or 3 minutes until bottom is golden brown. Turn carefully and cook for 1 or 2 minutes. Serve immediately, garnished with lemon wedges and parsley.

Domestically (farm) grown catfish are absolutely delicious.

SERVES 3–4.

STUFFED CALAMARI

This is great on pasta!

1 cup seasoned bread crumbs
2 tablespoons grated nonfat cheese
1 teaspoon oregano
1 teaspoon thyme
1 egg
1 pound fresh or frozen calamari, cleaned and washed
2 cups marinara sauce
2 tablespoons chopped fresh basil

In a bowl, mix bread crumbs, cheese, oregano, thyme and egg. Using a wide funnel, push about 1 tablespoon stuffing into each calamari.

Heat marinara sauce in medium saucepan until bubbling. Add stuffed calamari and cook in sauce for about 30 minutes.

Add fresh basil and serve as is or over pasta, or just as is with salad and hot Italian bread so you can sop up the sauce.

Hmmm.

You can also serve this with rice, mashed or baked potato, and a vegetable.

SERVES 4.

DOM'S STEAMED GINGER FISH

SAUCE:

2 tablespoons mild soy sauce
2 teaspoons rice wine
2 teaspoons olive oil

Combine the above for sauce.

1 pound fresh fish (red snapper, sea bass, sole)
3 scallions, cut lengthwise shredded fresh ginger

Wash fish and place in a small bowl. Split the scallions and cut into 3-inch sections. Pour sauce mixture all over the fish. Sprinkle the scallions and ginger on fish. Steam fish over boiling water in a bamboo steamer for about 12 minutes.

Serve immediately with lemon wedges.

SERVES 4–5.

That's me and Captain Chris Bock of Jupiter, Florida, filleting our catch.

The Bushes

I was in Washington doing publicity for *All Dogs Go to Heaven* and I was on the "Larry King Show." The publicity guy said that the White House knew I was in town and invited me to dinner. "Great! How wonderful!" I thought. So I finished with Larry King and I arrived at the White House a little late and went up the stairs to where everyone was already seated. I asked the escort, "Do you think I'll get to talk to Mrs. Bush?" He said, "You're sitting next to her." I said, "Wow, that's great." I really like her. So when I arrived I said hello to everyone at the table and I sat next to Mrs. Bush, who said, "Where the hell have you been?" I said, "The only reason I'm late for the President is because I was with a King. Larry King." She was trying to encourage young people to read and I've written children's books, *Charlie the Caterpillar* and a version of *Goldilocks,* so we talked about that for a while. The dinner was in honor of the French-speaking president from the Dominican Republic. So President Bush gave a speech and then this man with a French accent gave a speech. I said to Mrs. Bush, "Do you think it would be all right if I took out my Flashmatic camera?" She said, "I don't care what you take out." All the photographers had gone away and I took a picture of the President who was a table away and the flash made everybody's head turn. Then I thought, "Gee, wouldn't it be nice if I had a picture with Mrs. Bush?" So I asked a foreign dignitary wearing a pill box hat across from us if he would take a picture. I said, speaking slowly and articulately, "Do you think you could take a picture of me and Mrs. Bush?" He said, "Yeah, man," and I thought, "That's great, he speaks English very well." I posed with Mrs. Bush and he took two pictures and after I retrieved the camera and sat back down I said, "He was very nice. He made no fuss and he spoke English perfectly." Mrs. Bush said, "He should. That's Dizzy Gillespie." I said, "Oh my God. Dizzy Gillespie is great. I love him!" I gave the camera to a lady on my left and said, "Take a picture of me and Dizzy Gillespie." You can imagine how annoying I can be at the White House. Then we all walked around and the President was having some espresso and I said to him, "President Bush, I absolutely adore your wife." He said,

"Get in line." Then I asked Dizzy Gillespie to take a picture of me with the President and his demitasse. So all in all if I don't have my camera to remind me of who I am with, I wouldn't be able to recall these Kodak moments.

*E*very year about 3,000 Italians get together and honor a few select Italian Americans. This was particularly exciting because President Bush was going to be there. I was sent an invitation to sit on the dais and they were going to honor Ernest Borgnine. There were a lot of security men with dark suits and curled spaghetti wire coming out of their ears. I was on the dais sitting directly behind the President. I was trying to casually have Carol dine with me at the dais for a little while so

she could meet the
President. I caught
Carol's eye and with
my finger and a series
of signals I had her
walk to the right and I
walked to the right so
we could meet. When I
tried to get Carol onto
the dais I was informed
it would be impossible.
She was disappointed
but went back to her
seat. I guess because
John Wilkes Booth was
an actor and obviously
not to be trusted, they

were having second thoughts about my running around the dais loose. I
went up to one of the guards and tried to explain that Carol was harmless
and very excited at the possibility of
meeting the President and that I would
be a big man in my house if he helped
me accomplish this. He talked into his
chest for a while and I could see all the
security guards discussing this over to
the right and back at the door. They
must have had a network of communi-
cation. Finally a very serious gentle-
man came to me and said, "Please
come with me." I said, "Holy mackerel,
I'm being asked to leave." So I followed him reluctantly as we made our
way from the dais into the section
with the tables. He had me point
Carol out and she obediently stood
up with her lips pressed together
and her eyes widening. The three of
us went to the dais and approached

the Bushes who were extremely gracious! I took a picture with Carol and
Mrs. Bush. They were very kind because they were eating (not broccoli).
And stopped for us. People do this to me sometimes but I figured this
opportunity would not show itself again. Then I asked the President if I
could introduce him to my wife. He met Carol and I asked, "Is it okay if I
take a picture?" He said, warmly putting his arm around Carol, "Should we
trust him, Carol? Do you think Dom knows how to use that thing?" Carol
smiled as I flashed the picture and returned to my place on the dais like a
happy schoolboy. It's not simple because there's protocol and rules and
people with little wires coming out of their ears. You know what Gertrude
Stein said, "A moment is a moment is a moment," and I grabbed it. So, to
Bush or not to Bush was the question and I forged ahead and Bushed.

DOM'S BROCCOLI, WOOF!

Good enough to eat.

This will please everyone except President Bush.

2   *bunches broccoli, about 2 pounds, cut into
     florets*
4   *tablespoons lemon juice*
4   *tablespoons olive oil*
2   *teaspoons grated nonfat cheese*

Place broccoli in a pot filled with two inches of water. Bring water to a boil, then cover and simmer approximately 3 to 4 minutes, until just tender. Remove broccoli and place in a serving dish.

Pour lemon juice, olive oil and grated cheese over broccoli, mix well, and serve. Warm broccoli salad, also very good cold.

SERVES 6.

Note: This is also good with cauliflower florets, string beans or practically any other combination.

GREEN BEANS WITH STEWED TOMATOES

My cousin Tessie loved these.

3   *tablespoons chopped onion*
3   *garlic cloves, crushed*
2   *tablespoons olive oil*
1   *pound green beans, cut into 1-inch pieces*
1   *15-oz. can stewed tomatoes*
1/4 *teaspoon pepper*

In a medium saucepan, sauté onion and garlic in oil until golden brown. Add green beans, then stewed tomatoes and pepper.

Bring to a boil, then cover and simmer 30 minutes, stirring from time to time.

SERVES 6.

OPTIONAL: Add 1 peeled and diced potato when you sauté the onion and garlic.

Note: You can replace green beans with one pound of asparagus.

ACORN SQUASH

Good any time, any place. Like roasted.

1 *acorn squash*
    pepper to taste

Cut squash in half and remove seeds. Place squash halves in a greased baking dish. Bake at 350 degrees for about 1 hour. Serve in the shell. Or scoop out the flesh, mash and place in a bowl and serve.

    Or: Put 1 tablespoon butter and 1 tablespoon brown sugar inside each hollowed-out shell. Cover and bake for 1 hour.

    Or: The best: Clean and cut in eighths. Spray aluminum foil that has been placed on baking sheet. Place in oven and roast for about 25 minutes. It's quite the tasty treat. The skin is edible.

SERVES 2.

SPINACH CORN SOUFFLÉ

This is okay. Trust me—It works!

1 *8¹/₂-oz. package corn muffin mix*
4 *eggs, beaten (or equivalent or egg whites)*
1 *10¹/₂-oz. can cream of mushroom soup*
1 *14-oz. can cream-style corn*
1 *cup nonfat mozzarella, shredded (or American cheese, shredded)*
1 *10-oz. package frozen chopped spinach, thawed (or 2 cups leftover spinach)*
   pepper to taste

Place muffin mix in a large mixing bowl. Add the rest of the ingredients. Mix well.

Grease a large baking dish. Pour the soufflé mixture into the baking dish. Bake at 300 degrees about 1 hour, until golden brown on top.

Remove from the oven and let sit for 25 minutes before serving.

Great for buffets.

SERVES 8–10.

Pavarotti

orking at the Metropolitan Opera House in New York is a splendid way to spend December, Christmas, New Year's and January in New York City. Joe Volpe, the managing director of the Met, has invited me now for four different seasons to play Frosch in *Die Fledermaus* by Johann Strauss. As a child, listening to opera was a thrill and as I became a teenager I was enriched by the sounds of Callas, Caruso, Renata Tebaldi, Ezio Pinza and Feruccio Tagliavini, so it was no small wonder that I was thrilled out of my gourd when I got a call to be at the Met for the season. Working with opera singers is an awesome proposition because they're all incredibly talented and they're quite casual about their phenomenal skill. So you get to deal with them on a day-to-day basis and it's hard not to be impressed by their accomplishments. They love to laugh and in fact are very hardworking to say the least. Often a production will be mounted with people who live in Los Angeles, Germany, Belgium, England, France or Italy and they join together for December to work together in an opera. Frosch is a character who appears in the third act and it's rather like a tour de force for a comedian. Even when originally done in Strauss's time the part was played by a local comedian who contributed a lot of his own comic ideas and made a comical comment on the day especially in the political arena. My predecessors have been Cyril Ritchard, Sid Caesar and Jack Gilford (a dear friend of mine; when he came to see the production it took him an hour and a half to tell Carol and me, and all our guests, exactly what he did in his production).

When I was doing *Die Fledermaus*, the tenor sang and I ad-libbed one night. "That's very good, but here, take this," as I placed a long white handkerchief in his hand that I had pulled from my pocket. "Here. Take this. I gave it to a friend of mine and he does very well by it. Just let it hang there." I would hold his hand and stroke the handkerchief and it usually got a tremendous laugh because I was implying that he should hold the handkerchief that is part of Pavarotti's traditional stance. The second year we did *Die Fledermaus*, Joe Volpe had a surprise for me and on the closing night of the opera when I took out the handkerchief (I had no idea that this was going to happen) the upstage doors opened and two turn-of-the-century policemen came in accompanied by Pavarotti who shouted,

"Arrest him! Arrest him! He's impersonating me!" The audience responded with cheers, laughter, applause and as he came center stage, the tenor said, "What do you want?" I said, pointing to Pavarotti, "You mean you know this guy?" Then I looked at him with a second look. "Oh my God, it's my brother." And we embraced. He then said, "I have a proclamation." He took out a scroll and as he began to read it I said, grabbing a nearby chair and sitting on it, "Wait, wait. Your tickets are so expensive I don't want to miss one thing." He read a proclamation in essence that said I would be paid any salary I demanded and that I could, as long as he wasn't per-

forming it, play any roll I wanted. I said, "I'll have a kaiser roll." As he handed me the proclamation, we embraced again and there was gigantic applause as he exited. The opera continued and then during the curtain call I usually had a white handkerchief and I would mimic his curtain call. He joined me in my curtain call so that we were holding hands each holding a giant handkerchief. Part of my routine was that I had hidden in my handkerchief a wire hanger so after we bowed I slowly raised my handkerchief so the point of it went toward the ceiling. The cheering and "Bravos" helped top off an evening that I will never forget in my lifetime and has been one of the highlights of my career. Very wonderful to think about if I need any kind of boost. I just have to send my brain to that little trip when Luciano and Dom held hands on the stage of the Met and the only thing I could hear was the little boy that lived in my heart saying, "Wowee!"

STUFFED EGGPLANT (VEGETARIAN)

I think my mom invented this. I do know it's great!

1 *eggplant*
3 *tablespoons olive oil*
2 *garlic cloves, minced*
4 *mushrooms, chopped*
1 *medium onion,*
   chopped
1 *stalk celery, chopped*
2 *eggs*
2 *tablespoons chopped*
   parsley
   grated cheese
1 *cup grated mozzarella*
1 *cup marinara sauce*

(opposite)
Mel Brooks,
the funniest
and kindest
man I know,
and my
mamma.

Cut eggplant in half lengthwise; do not peel. Hollow out center of eggplant and set aside. Parboil hollowed-out halves for about 6 to 8 minutes.

Meanwhile, chop the eggplant center. In a large frying pan combine olive oil, eggplant center, garlic, mushrooms, onion and celery. Sauté until translucent. Transfer to a mixing bowl. Add eggs and parsley. Mix well.

Fill eggplant sections halfway with cooked mixture. Sprinkle with grated cheese. If desired, place 3 tablespoons of mozzarella in each eggplant center. Add remaining stuffing and top with remaining mozzarella, marinara sauce and more grated cheese. Place in a baking dish and bake at 350 degrees for 1 hour.

Excellent with chicken, fish, pasta or as a vegetarian meal with rice and a salad. The next day this makes a terrific cold buffet addition.

SERVES 4.

EGGPLANT ROLL-UPS

Great today, with pasta. Great tomorrow, cold in a sandwich.

1   *pound lowfat ricotta*
1   *tablespoon finely chopped parsley*
1   *large eggplant*
2   *eggs, beaten*
1   *cup seasoned bread crumbs*
1/3 *cup olive oil*
1/2 *pound nonfat mozzarella, shredded*
2   *cups marinara sauce*
1/2 *cup grated nonfat cheese*

Mix ricotta with parsley. Peel and thinly slice eggplant lenthwise. Dip each slice of eggplant into beaten eggs, then dip in bread crumbs.

Add oil to a Teflon frying pan over medium heat. Brown eggplant slices on both sides. Remove eggplant from pan and place on paper towels to drain.

Place 2 spoonfuls of ricotta mixture into the center of each eggplant slice. Add mozzarella and roll up eggplant slice around cheese. Place each roll seam side down in a shallow baking dish. Top with a little marinara sauce and grated cheese. Bake at 350 degrees for 35 minutes.

Serve with pasta and additional sauce, grated cheese and a salad.

SERVES 6.

BROCCOLI RABE OR SPINACH OR ESCAROLE

My mom used to make them this way and it is definitely worth the extra trouble.

Broccoli rabe is a slightly bitter green. It is greatly loved by most Italians that I know. I was doing a nightclub act at Resorts International in Atlantic City and when I introduced my 80-year-old mother, the audience applauded. But when I told them my mother came to the show with a jar of broccoli rabe, they not only applauded, they whistled and cheered!

Any questions?

2   *bunches broccoli rabe, cleaned (or 2 bunches spinach, cleaned, or*
     2 small heads escarole, coarsely chopped)
4   *tablespoons olive oil*
4   *garlic cloves, minced*
1/2 *cup chicken broth*
     lemon wedges
     grated cheese

Wash your green vegetable thoroughly (cut off the stems) and put aside. Boil water in large pot and blanch greens. Get a Teflon pan ready with olive oil and sauté garlic gently. In the meantime throw the greens in the boiling water and cook for about 1 to 2 minutes. Use a pair of tongs to remove the greens and drop them in the pan with the oil and garlic. When all the greens have been transferred, add chicken broth, cover and cook for about 3 to 4 minutes (spinach about 1 minute).

Serve with lemon wedges and grated cheese.

This keeps the color green and the taste great!

Small portions of this are to be served.

SERVES 6–8.

Optional: Add a 12 oz. can of cannellini beans to finished dish. Heat gently and eat.

STUFFED RED PEPPERS

Hello Middle America.

1/2 pound ground turkey
2 garlic cloves, minced
1 onion, minced
2 tablespoons olive oil
2 cups whole kernel corn (or 1 15-oz. can corn, drained)
3/4 cup seasoned bread crumbs
2 eggs
4 tablespoons ketchup
6 medium red peppers
1 cup tomato juice
6 tablespoons shredded nonfat mozzarella cheese

In a medium saucepan, brown turkey, garlic and onion in oil.

In a mixing bowl, combine browned turkey, onion, corn, bread crumbs, eggs and ketchup.

Cut pepper in half lengthwise. Remove seeds and membranes, then parboil peppers for 3 minutes.

Fill peppers with tukey mixture and set each pepper in a baking dish. Pour tomato juice in the bottom of the baking dish and some on top of the peppers. Sprinkle peppers with grated mozzarella.

Cover with foil and bake at 350 degrees for 1 hour.

SERVES 6.

LAVONNE'S ARMENIAN VEGETABLES OR "TOUR LU"

Carol and I have a lot of wonderful friends in Vermont. We are especially fond of John and Wini Hawkes. Carol has known them since she was 15 years old so we go back a long time with them. John plays tennis every day and has the disposition of a young boy. His wife, Wini, a very special lady, is the town facilitator and she has single-handedly created a library with self-help books for all to use. Every time I have any kind of problem, I simply call my friend Wini from wherever I am in the world. She always helps me solve whatever my problems, then (Wini being the dispenser of humor) I aways get to hear at least two of the latest jokes before I hang up.

Carol and I, along with Wini and John, were invited to dine at the home of Paul and LaVonne Robinson. They are both expert weavers and met 30 years ago when they were just learning to use the loom. It's great to visit them because there are two big looms in their house and looms are not small, but their size seems to represent the magnitude of Paul and LaVonne's love for each other. It's very sweet.

LaVonne cooked a delicious meatless meal. This vegetarian feast, absolutely delicious, was served to us with Paul's famous homemade bread. Paul is in his eighties and he and I often make bread together. We have a ball listening to jazz, laughing a lot, and having more fun than a barrel of monkeys. He is a wonderful man and truly I love him almost as much as I love his bread.

LaVonne served a crisp, fresh salad with an olive oil and lemon dressing. Everybody had three helpings. The meal was topped off with lemon sherbet and everybody was so mellow afterward, we talked till dawn and solved the problems of the entire universe.

Truly a delicious evening.

SAUCE:

1	28-oz. can cut-up tomatoes
1/2	cup ketchup
1/2	cup olive oil
1	teaspoon sugar
1/2	cup cut-up fresh basil
	black pepper to taste

1	eggplant, with skin, cut into bite-size pieces
2	onions, cut in chunks
2	carrots, peeled and sliced
2	stalks celery, sliced into 1/2-inch pieces
1	small red pepper, cut into bite-size pieces
1	small green pepper
1	cup corn
1 1/2	cups green beans, cut into 2-inch pieces
3–4	red potatoes, peeled and cut into bite-size pieces
8–10	mushrooms, cut into quarters

In a large casserole combine tomatoes, ketchup, oil, sugar, basil and pepper. Add all the vegetables and mix gently.

Cover and place in 350-degree oven for 1 1/2 hours. Uncover and cook another 15 to 20 miutes. During the last 15 to 20 minutes, if you want to add a cup of sliced zucchini, that is optional. When reheating leftovers, LaVonne says she adds a little cheese on top! M-m-m.

SERVES 8–10. EXPECT LEFTOVERS.

Note: This vegetable can be served with any fish, meat or fowl you wish to enhance. A flavor to die for. Simple, so delicious . . . Stand back!

Ralph the Fruit and Vegetable Man and His Horse Nellie

When I was a kid, our family lived in Brooklyn and often the street vendors were local people who had a business that they operated from a horse-drawn wagon. I remember there was a vegetable man named Ralph and he would sell vegetables from a horse-drawn wagon. My mother would buy vegetables from him and I would watch the horse chewing its lunch. Fascinating! Sometimes when I'm in the supermarkets of today I flashback on the little boy who was so impressed that there was a whole horse to pull those few fruits and vegetables from street to street so Ralph could sell his wares. My mother would pick this tomato, those carrots, that eggplant, and I'd go home feeling as if I had just had an adventure.

I remember when Ralph's horse jumped over a fence and ran down the block. All of us kids were very excited because we had our very own runaway horse. Ralph and his sons ran this way and that, but Nellie avoided them all. It didn't take long before a large crowd gathered. My mom and dad came to see. She and I stood on the stoop while my father went out into the street, and I thought to myself, "Doesn't he see the runaway horse coming right at him?" "Watch out, John!" my mother shouted. And then my father, who worked for the Department of Sanitation, reached out with his arms and embraced the horse's neck as it approached him. My father was dragged by the horse. Grabbing hold of the reins, my father pulled himself up and bit the horse's right ear. The horse stopped very quickly, jerking his head. And it was my father's bold move that had indeed done it. There was applause, and Ralph and his sons came

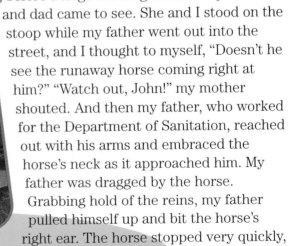

Papa John, Mamma Jenny, brother Nick, sister Anne and me.

quickly to harness Nellie and return her to the wagon.

I had been to the movies, so I knew what a hero was. Usually they rescue a child from a burning building, but never had I seen a hero in the movies save the day by biting the ear of a horse. At this writing, Mike Tyson was disqualified in a fight with the World Heavyweight Champion, Evander Holyfield, for biting Holyfield's ears. Not once but twice, once on each ear. The response from the media and sports world was horrendous for Tyson, who was fined $3,000,000 and banned, possibly for life, from boxing in Nevada.

Now it seems to me that if you bite a runaway horse on the ear once, then you're a hero. However, it seems inadvisable to bite a contender for the heavyweight championship of the world on each ear in the same fight. There's a moral to this story: Don't bite when you fight, but you might get away with biting a horse on the ear, if you just gotta!

To me, it was exciting to have the horse-ear biting incident spice up my impressionable youth. My father told the story over and over again. Each time the horse got bigger and so did my father's head. The Tyson biting incident has left a bad taste in everybody's mouth. As for me, I'm going to remain neutral and just keep biting fruits and vegetables and more than I can chew.

My Confirmation. That's my brother, "Nick the Prince." He was my hero.

Rice and Potatoes

AZMINA'S INCREDIBLE PARTY RICE DISH

I have a friend named Gene Vladimir Czaplinsky. I love him very much. We've known each other 25 years and I cherish his friendship. When Gene was a small boy, he and his family came to America and made a life here. Gene is a very handsome man and he married a beautiful woman, Azmina, from Uganda. They have produced this incredible child, Sasha. Gene and Azmina are a wonderful combination. Not only is Azmina gorgeous, but she is also a fabulous cook. Exotic, delicious and fast! Even faster than me! She recently came to a party with this dish. I love rice and this is "feastive" and a winner. So enjoy!

1	*cup basmati rice*
1	*cup wild rice*
6	*garlic cloves, minced*
1	*large onion, minced*
4	*tablespoons olive oil*
2	*tomatoes, diced*
1/2	*teaspoon cumin*
1/2	*teaspoon coriander powder*
1/2	*teaspoon paprika*
1 1/2	*teaspoons turmeric*
1/2	*cup cilantro, chopped*
1/2	*cup each of sesame seeds, pine nuts, raisins, dried cranberries, chopped dates and chopped almonds*

Soak basmati rice in water and put aside. In a pot, put wild rice and one quart of water. Bring to a boil, lower to simmer, cover pot, and cook for 45 minutes. Drain basmati rice and add to wild rice. Cook another 10 minutes on medium heat. Drain rice. Place in large casserole dish.

Sauté garlic and onion in oil for 3 minutes and add to casserole along with the rest of the ingredients. Mix well and bake in a preheated 350-degree oven for 10 minutes. Let cool, and serve.

This can be served with shrimp, chicken, fish, turkey, pork and beef. Enjoy!

SERVES 20–25.

Gene and Azmina are very successful entrepreneurs. They work with officials in Russia and the Ukraine. They visit with Gorbachev and say he is pleasant, warm and funny. Azmina must have made him her rice dish. Or else how come he's so nice?

SPANISH RICE

Ole!

3 tablespoons olive oil
1 garlic clove, minced
1 red or green pepper, chopped
1 onion, chopped
1 stalk celery, chopped
8 mushrooms, sliced
1 cup rice
4 cups tomato juice
1/2 cup grated cheese
2 tablespoons chopped parsley

Add oil to a medium frying pan. Cook garlic, pepper, onion, celery and mushrooms over medium heat until garlic is lightly browned and onions are translucent. Mix in rice and tomato juice.

Grease a 1^{1}/$_{2}$-quart casserole. Spread the rice and vegetable mixture in the casserole. Cover and bake at 350 degrees for about 45 minutes, until the rice is tender and the liquid has been absorbed. Uncover and stir. Sprinkle grated cheese on top. Place casserole back in oven, uncovered, for about 5 minutes, until golden brown on top.

Garnish with parsley and serve.

SERVES 6.

Robert Clary

I met Robert many years ago when we were in a show called *Around the World in Eighty Days*. He was a perfect Passepartout and was famous for being so wonderful in *New Faces of 1952* (seems like a hundred years ago). I played Mr. Fix, and Robert and I became friends and we have stayed friends all these years. He and his lovely wife, Natalie (one of Eddie Cantor's daughters), have been happily married for a long time.

I love Robert for a lot of reasons. He is as serious as you need him to be. My son Michael, at school, was once told by a teacher that the Holocaust did not exist, that it was a hoax! I called Robert, who is a survivor of the Holocaust. He quickly arranged to be the speaker at my son's school and handled the situation with great class. And then, of course, his ever-present child is always available; Robert is more fun than a barrel of monkeys, and I love him for that!

I get a smile every time I look at this picture.

Carol and I see Robert and Natalie very often and recently he sang at The Jazz Bakery, here in Los Angeles. Carol and I were, of course, there! I was thrilled because he is a brilliant singer-entertainer, and I am so proud to know him. Then Robert had another showing of his artwork.

Robert and me at his art show. That's me on the right!

Well, I am thrilled *again.* Burt Reynolds had been the proud owner of "Robert's art" and Carol and I are now the proud owners of two pieces. Robert works in colored pencils and the results are awesome, fabulous, make-me-crazy beautiful.

This picture belongs to Burt Reynolds.

I also think that Robert and I look amazingly good together. From me, the ridiculous, to Robert, the sublime. My sweet, talented friend, Robert Clary, ooh-la-la!

Whenever we have dinner together Robert is so amusing because he tells the best stories. He is a raconteur personified. The last time we were together I remember he ordered rabbit. *Sacre bleu!*

Carol and I love our "Venice Back Alley" picture.

DOM'S FRIEND EVE'S KASHA VARNISHKES

Eve Roberts and I have been friends since I was 18 years old and she is a very fine actress, a great mother and a million laughs. But the laughter stops when she cooks. She makes baked salmon and you want to leave home. She also brought kasha varnishkes to a potluck we had at our house and when nobody was looking I hid some of it for later. It's good, tasty and this is it—oh boy!

A taste you dream of.

1   cup minced onion
4   tablespoons olive oil
2   cups cooked kasha (follow
    directions on box and use
    chicken broth)
3   cups bow tie pasta, cooked al
    dente
    pepper to taste

Brown the onions in the oil. In a bowl combine kasha, onion, pasta and pepper. Mix well.

Serve hot. Ah, but the next day it's even better cold.

SERVES 6–8.

RISOTTO

Rice . . . is nice!

3   tablespoons olive oil or butter
1   medium onion, finely chopped
1 1/2   cups rice (Italian Arborio rice is best)
3–4   cups chicken broth, heated
        pinch saffron
1/2   cup white wine
        pepper to taste
1/4   cup grated Parmesan cheese

In a large, heavy saucepan, sauté onion in oil or butter until onion is translucent. Add rice and sauté briefly until rice is coated with oil. Add about 1 cup hot chicken broth to rice. Stir until broth is almost absorbed. Continue adding chicken broth 1/2 cup at a time as the rice absorbs the broth (this will take 15 to 20 minutes). Do not allow the rice to stick to the bottom of the pan.

Crush the saffron and dissolve it in the white wine. Add the white wine to rice. At this point, the rice should be thick, but not watery. Add the pepper and Parmesan cheese to the rice mixture and mix thoroughly.

Place the rice mixture in a serving bowl and garnish with parsley.

SERVES 6.

OPTIONAL: After adding the wine, try adding any of the following ingredients:

1/2 cup cooked sausage, chopped, and 1/2 cup mushrooms, chopped
1/2 cup red and 1/2 cup green peppers, chopped
1/2 cup walnuts, chopped, and 1/2 cup diced asparagus

The Wedding Band

I did a movie called *The Wedding Band,* which was written and directed by Martin Guigui in Burlington, Vermont. I played a priest and I really had a wonderful time! I am happy to say I met Vinny and Margaret Anne Vella, and their son Vinny Jr.—and it was like I was suddenly talking to relatives. Vinny is a really wonderful natural actor and he played the godfather at an Italian-Jewish wedding. He was so natural you had the feeling you were there. Every time he would perform he was really terrific. He has done lots of work with Robert De Niro and did a great job in *Casino.* We were all sitting around talking about food; why, I'll never know! Anyway, I realized that I hadn't made rice balls for a long time. Margaret Anne and Vinny along with Sal and Marie Piro and I talked about rice balls. It started to rain and we all just sat there and talked. We had a lot of laughs. We will all probably meet next year and talk about veal.

DOM'S FRIENDS, MARGARET ANNE AND VINNY'S RICE BALLS

    2   cups cooked rice (Italian or regular), cooled
    4   eggs, beaten
    1   cup grated Parmesan cheese
    1   cup minced fresh parsley
         pepper to taste
    4   egg whites, beaten
         flavored bread crumbs
         olive-oil spray

FOUR FILLINGS TO PUT IN THE CENTER OF RICE BALLS:

1   *cup diced mozzarella*
1   *cup ricotta*
4   *slices prosciutto, diced*

2   *teaspoons olive oil*
2   *garlic cloves, minced*
     chopped meat or sausage
1   *onion, chopped*
1/2   *cup tomato paste*
1   *cup peas*

Sauté garlic, meat, onion,
add pasta and peas.

Margaret, Michael, me, Vinny and Tina.

1   *piece mozzarella*
1   *piece prosciutto*

2   *teaspoons olive oil*
2   *garlic cloves, minced*
1   *cup chopped spinach*
1   *cup ricotta*

Sauté garlic and spinach,
add ricotta.

In a large bowl place cooked rice, 4 eggs, cheese, parsley and pepper and mix well with a wooden spoon. Place about 3 teaspoons of the mixture in your hand and make a small pocket with your finger and put about 1 teaspoon of one of the above mixtures and add a teaspoon more of the rice mixture. Touch your fingers to the egg whites as you roll the rice in your hand into a ball. Since your fingers have been applying the egg mixture to the outside of the rice balls, you can then roll them in the flavored bread crumbs to coat the entire ball. Place aside.

Traditionally these rice balls are fried in a little olive oil and gently turned until golden brown. I place them on a piece of greased foil that lines a large baking pan or cookie sheet and I then spray the rice balls with olive-oil spray and place them in a preheated 350-degree oven for about 35 minutes or until golden brown.

I love these rice balls. They are excellent hot. They're even good cold the next day—that is, if there are any left.

ONE BALL IS VERY FILLING. EXPECT 1 1/2 RICE BALLS PER PERSON.

FAT-FREE OVEN-FRIED POTATOES

All this and heaven too!

5 *large baking potatoes*
   vegetable oil cooking spray
2 *large egg whites*

Cut each potato crosswise into $1/2$-inch slices, then slice lengthwise into fingersticks.

Coat a baking sheet with vegetable oil spray.

In a large bowl combine the potatoes and egg whites and mix to coat. Pour the coated potatoes onto the prepared baking sheet and spread them out into a single layer, leaving space between each slice.

Place the baking sheet in a preheated 400-degree oven. Bake for 40 to 45 minutes or until the fries are crispy, turning them once with a spatula so that they brown evenly.

Serve immediately.

SERVES 5–8.

Charlie the Caterpillar

In 1973, when I submitted *Charlie the Caterpillar,* the first children's book I wrote, I got quite a few rejections. Just an encouraging word to anybody who's dreaming of being a writer. I didn't alter the manuscript at all, and at this writing I have written close to about ten books. I can only tell you that the rose smells just as sweet if you can get your nose near it.

DOM'S WHATEVER KNISHES

The Jewish style of cooking places a lot of emphasis on noodles, pancakes and dough. Like Italian or Chinese cuisine, a Jewish meal always has some kind of starch.

Knishes, always a great favorite, have become enormously popular in recent years as cocktail-party snacks. Of course, the modern version is daintier than the old, familiar knish. But it still tastes the same despite its streamlined appearance.

DOUGH:

2½   cups sifted flour
1   teaspoon baking powder
3   eggs
¼   cup oil
2   tablespoons water

Mix flour and baking powder in a bowl. Make a well in the center and drop eggs, oil and water into it. Work into the flour mixture with your hands and knead until smooth.

There are two ways to fill the knishes. In either case, divide the dough in two and roll as thin as possible. Brush with oil. Now you can spread the filling on one side of the dough and roll it up like a jelly roll. Tuck the sides under. Place in a greased baking sheet flap side down. Press the dough down lightly to flatten and bake at 350 degrees for 35 minutes, or until golden brown.

Or you can cut the rolled dough into 3-inch circles. Place 1 tablespoon of filling on each; draw the edges together and pinch firmly. Place on an oiled baking sheet, pinched edges up. Bake in a 375-degree oven 30 to 35 minutes, or until golden brown.

MAKES ABOUT 24.

I like to use wonton wrappers. In the middle of each wrapper put 1 teaspoon of filling and bring all the corners together and twist gently. Place on a greased cookie sheet in a 350-degree oven for 20 to 25 minutes, until golden brown.

Makes great hors d'oeuvres.

Various Fillings for Knishes

POTATO:

1 cup chopped onions
4 tablespoons oil
3 cups mashed potatoes
2 eggs
1/4 teaspoon pepper

Brown onions in the oil. Mix with potatoes, eggs and pepper until fluffy.

MAKES 8 KNISHES.

CHEESE-ONION:

1 1/2 cups diced onions
4 tablespoons oil
2 1/2 cups cottage cheese
2 eggs
1/8 teaspoon pepper
2 tablespoons sour cream

Brown onions in the oil and mix in the cheese, eggs, pepper and sour cream. Mix until smooth.

MAKES 8 KNISHES.

SWEET CHEESE:

3 cups cottage cheese
2 eggs
4 tablespoons sugar
1/2 teaspoon vanilla
2 tablespoons sour cream
    dash cinnamon (optional)

Combine all the ingredients and mix well.

MAKES 8 KNISHES.

MEAT:

1   *cup chopped onions*
2   *tablespoons olive oil*
1¹/₂   *cups chopped cooked*
        meat, beef, turkey
        or veal or leftovers
1³/₄   *cup cooked rice*
2   *eggs*
        pepper to taste

Brown onions in the
oil. Add the meat,
rice, eggs and pepper
and mix until smooth.

MAKES 8 KNISHES.

CHICKEN OR TURKEY:

1   *cup chopped onions*
2   *tablespoons oil*
2   *cups chopped cooked chicken*
        or turkey
1   *cup mashed potatoes*
2   *eggs*
¹/₄   *teaspoon pepper*

We have a lot in common except
for the tongue.

Brown onions in the oil. Add the chicken or turkey, potatoes, eggs and
pepper. Mix all ingredients until smooth.

MAKES 8 KNISHES.

POTATO-ONION-CORN:

1 *cup chopped onions*
4 *tablespoons oil*
2 *cups mashed potatoes*
1 *cup corn, drained*
2 *eggs*
  pepper to taste

Brown onions in the oil. Mix with the potatoes, corn, eggs and pepper.

Potato-Spinach:

1 cup chopped onions
4 tablespoons oil
2 cups mashed potatoes
1 cup chopped spinach
2 eggs
  pepper to taste

Brown onions in the oil. Mix with the potatoes, spinach, eggs and pepper.

Makes 8 knishes.

DOM'S POTATO PANCAKES

I tasted these delicious pancakes years ago and I asked how to make them. I was told to hand grate the potato and the onion. There was no other way. My knuckles did not agree. I now use a food processor or blender and I really enjoy the help.

2 eggs
3 cups (about 5) grated potatoes
1 tablespoon flour (or matzo meal or Bisquick)
1 onion, diced
1 teaspoon oil
  pepper to taste

In a large bowl, mix together the eggs, potatoes, and onion. In a Teflon pan over medium heat or on a grill, drop by the tablespoon the potato mixture and cook until golden brown on both sides (turning them of course!).

Remove to paper towels (to remove oil). Keep them hot. They are great with beef, chicken or fish. They love mustard and they love applesauce—not necessarily together!

Instead of, like scraping your knuckles, you can like, applaud with your hands!

Makes 35 or so pancakes, depending on how big your spoon is!

SPAETZLE (GERMAN DUMPLINGS)

We have a house in Vermont and our friends Rudy and June Gutbier had us over for a fabulous German dinner cooked by Rudy. June is in communications and hysterically funny. Rudy works in wood and I've seen him carve a little girl coming down the mountain with a sheep and a goat, flying a kite and picking flowers simultaneously. Not really, but his carving is so exquisite that's the feeling you get.

Fred and Pat Carmichael, who ran a theater in Vermont for many years, were with us. It was from Pat and Fred that my young wife Carol learned the ins and outs of theatrical life. Interestingly enough, Fred is now a full-time playwright and Pat works in wood. We were all having a very special, fun evening playing games and laughing a lot and I got very serious when Rudy served spaetzle with sauerbraten, something I had never tasted before and thought was very delicious, especially accompanying the sauerbraten. I'm sure there are many versions, but this recipe is unique and quite different. I for one think it's delicious and very special.

Thank you, Rudy.

3   cups flour
1/2 teaspoon baking powder
1   level teaspoon nutmeg
4   eggs
1   cup milk
4   tablespoons soft butter or oil

In a large bowl, combine flour, baking powder and nutmeg. Stir and then create a well to hold the eggs and milk. Knead into dough. Bring a half-filled large pot of water to a boil. The best way to do it is to buy a spaetzle maker from a gourmet shop or to use a large-holed greased colander. Holding the colander over the boiling water, force the dough mixture through the holes with a wooden spoon or spatula. Keep the water close to a boil as the pieces drop into the water becoming teardrop noodles. Then cook a couple of minutes, reducing the heat. When they all float to the top, they're done. I was trained to drain them in another colander, then to drop them in a cold water bath, which will prevent them from clinging together.

You can serve these by sautéing them in butter, adding cheese, pepper or parsley to taste. Or they're perfect with sauerbraten. Also, they're great tossed with spaghetti sauce and grated cheese or $1/2$ cup warm sour cream, bacon bits or turkey sausage. Use in stew, goulash, boiled beef and creamed chicken. Fry in a little butter and mix with scrambled eggs and cheese. Add to soup. Toss with grated cheese and butter. The possibilities are endless.

SERVES 6.

Cold Water Flat

The first time I lived away from home was in a cold water flat. The rent was $37 a month. My take-home pay was $37.50 and I was doing an off-Broadway show called Another Evening with Harry Stoones. Barbra Streisand was also in it. I lived in a cold water flat. This is an apartment that has no hallways and in which every room is connected As you enter, the front door has a giant bar that locks into place to keep out intruders. There's a stove, a kitchen sink and a bathtub. On the bathtub is a giant piece of wood that serves as a counter for when you're making dinner. In this particular flat there was a small room with a toilet and the other room served as a living room, dining room and an office.

There was a fireplace that was all sealed up years ago. It was cold so I decided to take the bricks out of it and make it functional. I ended up with thousands of bricks.The chimney was stacked with bricks, my apartment was full of bricks. Each time I left my apartment I took out eight bricks with me until they were all gone. It was so cold because between the bricks the mortar was gone and I could see clear through to the other building. At eight o'clock every morning I would make a baked potato, whether I wanted it or not, just to heat myself up. The windows were so loose, I lit a candle and had melted wax in the cracks to keep the wind out. I went to the dry cleaners, got lots of plastic wrap, nailed it over the windows and covered them with drapes. Even with all that, the plastic wrap would billow out in the wind. Taking a bath was a big production. I bathed in the same room where I cooked and entertained. When my sons grew up in our current house, they insisted that they each have their own bathroom. Oh, if only they knew.

Barbra

*B*arbra has always been exquisitely talented. We were both starting out and our dreams were young. Sheila Copeland, the girl on my left, was a very talented actress. She was in shows like *Two for the Seesaw* and *The Miracle Worker.* I loved her very much. We lost her when she was thirty. I miss her every day.

Barbra and her talent have achieved such incredible heights. When Barbra sings I have goose pimples that start on the heels of my feet and work their way up my spine and out through the top of my head. I think she's a great artist. Go, go. Fly high!

I am privileged to know her.

Pizza

BASIC PIZZA DOUGH

1 tablespoon dried yeast (1 package)
1 teaspoon sugar
1 cup warm water (more if necessary)
3 cups flour
1 tablespoon olive oil

Put yeast into a small bowl and add sugar
and warm water. Allow to stand for 5 min-
utes, then mix until smooth. Pour the yeast mixture into a large
bowl with the flour and olive oil. Mix with your hands to a stiff dough.
Knead on a floured board for 10 minutes. Use more water if necessary.

Place dough ball in an oiled bowl and put in a fairly warm place until it
has doubled in size. Punch down and reshape ball. (Repeat if you have time.)

Turn dough onto a floured board and roll dough to a thickness of $1/4$ inch. Place on baking sheet sprayed with olive oil.

Or: Process in a food processor using the plastic blade to make dough. It is amazingly fast and you can do the entire process in about $3^{1}/_{2}$ minutes.

MAKES TWO SMALL PIZZAS OR ONE LARGE 9-INCH PIZZA.

SUPER PIZZA

1   *medium onion, sliced into crescents*
1   *tablespoon olive oil*
1   *cup tomato sauce*
       Basic Pizza Dough (see page 192)
$1/2$ *pound cooked Italian sausage, chopped*
2   *slices cooked bacon, diced*
1   *red or green pepper, chopped*
8   *mushrooms, sliced*
       nonfat mozzarella cheese, shredded
       pepper to taste
       oregano

Sauté onion in olive oil in a saucepan until transparent. Add tomato sauce. Cook on low heat, uncovered, for about 15 minutes.

Roll out dough and spread on baking sheet sprayed with olive oil. Cover dough with sausage, bacon, pepper, mushrooms, cheese and season with pepper. Add cooked tomato sauce and sprinkle with oregano.

Bake in a 350-degree oven for about 25 to 35 minutes.

SERVES 4–6.

BROCCOLI-CHEESE PIZZA

Basic Pizza Dough (see page 192)
2   *garlic cloves, minced*
1   *cup broccoli, cut into bite-size pieces*
$^1/_4$ *cup chopped onion*
2   *tablespoons olive oil*
$^1/_2$ *cup shredded Cheddar cheese*

Place pizza bottom on a lightly greased pizza pan.

Sauté garlic, broccoli and onion in oil in a Teflon pan about 2 minutes. Spoon hot vegetable mixture over pizza bottom. Sprinkle with Cheddar cheese.

Bake at 350 degrees for 12 minutes, or until cheese is bubbly.

SERVES 4–6.

Note: For Tomato-Broccoli-Cheese Pizza add 1 cup tomato sauce to pizza bottom before broccoli mixture.

My wonderful son Peter worked in a pizza joint before he became an actor, writer and director.

GERMAN PIZZA (REUBEN)

Basic Pizza Dough *(see page 192)*
4   *tablespoons prepared Thousand Island salad dressing*
1   *cup canned corned beef, crumbled or sliced*
1   *cup sauerkraut, drained and squeezed dry*
1/2 *teaspoon caraway seed (optional)*
1   *cup Swiss cheese, shredded or sliced*

Place your pizza bottom on a lightly greased pizza pan.

Spread salad dressing over pizza bottom. Top with corned beef, sauerkraut, caraway seed and cheese.

Bake at 350 degrees for about 12 minutes, or until cheese is bubbly.

SERVES 8.

PIZZA NAPOLETANA

Basic Pizza Dough (see page 192)
2 *pounds canned Italian tomatoes, chopped pepper to taste*
1 *cup sliced nonfat mozzarella cheese*
$1/2$ *teaspoon oregano*
$1/2$ *teaspoon basil*
$1/2$ *cup black olives, pitted and sliced Parmesan cheese*

Place rolled out pizza dough on a baking sheet sprayed with olive oil. Spread tomatoes over dough and sprinkle with pepper. Arrange slices of mozzarella over tomatoes. Sprinkle with oregano and basil. Garnish with black olive slices and Parmesan cheese.

Bake at 350 degrees for about 30 minutes.

Note: This can magically become anchovy pizza simply by adding canned anchovies, cut into pieces.

SERVES 4–6.

Jason Priestley

I have been an actor for a lot of years now. I have almost taken it for granted that I will arrive at a movie shoot, check my costumes, say hello to the director, go to makeup and find out where the set is I'm going to shoot on. I recently got a call saying that I was wanted for "Beverly Hills 90210" and I really do like that show quite a bit. I was going to be working with Jason Priestley, whom I had met doing publicity for my book, *Goldilocks,* and I found him to be really warm. He knows my sons Peter, Michael and David, and I really admire his talent. When I got to the show, I was thrilled when I realized that Jason was so available, enthusiastic, and so pleasant that he turned work into a party. He's the producer of the show now.

I found myself standing on a floor that made a loud creaking noise if I even shifted my weight. So I said, "Don't worry. I'll stand with my legs wider apart." And he said, almost under his breath, "Not necessary. Can someone put some nails into the floor so that Mr. DeLuise doesn't have to concentrate on creaking boards?" We went to have a glass of water and in three minutes the floor didn't creak anymore. Then later, in the second scene, I was surprised to be on the telephone talking to him, when he very easily could have gone home and had the script girl read his lines. But he very graciously volunteered to stay. I was a little dense and kept screwing up, so we took more time than was probably necessary, but he was there being supportive and validating and with great humor, and I was very touched.

"Beverly Hills 90210" has been on a very long time and after you do something for years and years, you sometimes just are there connecting the dots and getting to go home is the priority of the day. Not so with Jason. He was so pleasant and available, when I have seen too many stars, especially young ones, not care. He treated me terrific and made me feel special. I regret that we didn't take a picture together, but when I called him up to ask him for a photo to use in this book, he sent it by messenger and referred to me as a king in the picture. So Jason Priestley, you got one more fan for life. I'm older and wiser and balder than some of the young fans but I'm just as crazy about you as they are!

COLD SALMON (OR LOX) PIZZA

Basic Pizza Dough (see page 192)
2   *teaspoons olive oil*
4   *garlic cloves, minced*
1   *8-oz. package lowfat cream cheese, softened*
4   *tablespoons finely chopped onion*
1   *tablespoon chopped fresh parsley*
     pepper to taste
1   *8-oz. can salmon, drained and flaked*
¹/₂ *teaspoon dill weed*
2   *tablespoons capers*

Place your pizza bottom on a lightly greased pizza pan.

In a bowl combine oil and garlic. Spread mixture over your pizza bottom. Bake at 375 degrees for about 12 minutes, or until crust is golden brown. Cool.

In a small bowl, combine cream cheese, onion, parsley and pepper. Spread over cooled crust.

Top with salmon and capers and sprinkle with dill weed. Add tomato slices and onion rings. Cut into wedges and serve. This dish can be refrigerated.

SERVES 8.

Note: Salmon can be replaced with slices of lox. Excellent!

CALZONE

A calzone is simply a pizza folded in half like a turnover. I use the same dough for calzone. They are fun to prepare and you can use any combination of fillings you prefer. Let everyone in your family create their own "personalized" stuffed pizza at home.

Suggested fillings:

MEATS
Italian sausage
hamburger
pepperoni
salami
Canadian bacon
ham

CHEESES
mozzarella
Monterey Jack
Cheddar
Swiss
Parmesan

FISH
salmon
shrimp
smoked oysters
tuna

VEGETABLES
onions
peppers
zucchini
asparagus
garlic
tomatoes
mushrooms
broccoli

My mother Vincenza and her great-granddaughter Vincenza making calzone together.

A calzone and me.

Me and my star pupil, Katie Adams.

CALZONE

A pocket full of joy!

2 cups nonfat ricotta cheese
1 cup shredded nonfat mozzarella, Cheddar or American cheese
1 cup cooked, chopped vegetables (broccoli, onions, spinach, etc.)
Basic Pizza Dough (see page 192)

In a bowl, mix together the cheeses and vegetables. Divide dough into two batches. Roll dough to about 1/4 inch thick and place on a greased baking pan. Fill with half the cheese and vegetable mixture. Fold dough over and pinch edges together tightly. With a scissors, snip three small holes in top for air. Repeat for the second calzone.

Bake at 350 degrees for about 45 to 60 minutes, until top is golden brown. It's ready when the sides bubble.

MAKES 2 CALZONES; SERVES 2.

OPTIONAL: You can also add meat fillings (try 3 slices of cut-up ham) and different cheeses (2 teaspoons of grated cheese).

Bruno's Pizzeria

*T*here is a pizzeria in Manchester, Vermont, called Bruno's. However, Mario owns and runs it. He is a great cook (in his sleep). He is just really good at what he does. His wife, Marilyn, is a terrific lady and we always have a lot of laughs whenever our family goes there. Mario makes a lot of great veal dishes, pizza and calzone to die for! If I was going to be on a deserted island with only one person I would bring Mario just in case I felt faint. You know!

Mario once gave me a pizza screen so that the pizza gets crispy on the bottom and it works like gangbusters.

It was snowing at Bruno's so the pizza tasted even better!

My friends, Mario and his wonderful wife, Marilyn.

BASIC DOUGH

An excellent pizza or bread dough. Also great for calzones and rolls, or cheese and onion bread.

3 *cups unbleached flour*
1 *package granulated yeast*
1 *teaspoon sugar*
1/2 teaspoon oil
3/4 cup warm water (slightly more or less as needed)

Combine dry ingredients in a large bowl. Add oil, then pour water slowly into dry ingredients. Mix, then knead until fully blended into a workable dough.

Note: This works great in a food processor. Mix sugar and yeast together first in the warm water, then add to the flour and oil in the food processor. Add water as needed. Fast and perfect.

Place dough in a large greased bowl. Cover with a towel and set aside in a warm place. In 2 hours it will double in size. Knead again. The dough is now ready to use for pizza. For bread, shape into loaves, let rise again, then bake.

SERVES 4.

BRAN MUFFINS

What's wrong? These will keep you right!

1	cup boiling water
1	cup 100% bran
$1/2$	stick margarine
$1^1/2$	cups brown sugar
1	pint buttermilk
2	eggs, beaten
2	cups All-Bran cereal
$2^1/2$	cups flour
$2^1/2$	teaspoons baking soda
$1/2$	cup chopped nuts (optional)
$1/2$	cup raisins (optional)

In a large mixing bowl, combine boiling water, bran and margarine. Add sugar, buttermilk, eggs, All-Bran, flour and baking soda. Mix well. Add nuts and raisins (optional).

Pour into a greased 12-muffin tin. Bake at 350 degrees for 20 to 25 minutes.

MAKES 25–30 LARGE MUFFINS.

OLD ENGLISH HOT CROSS BUNS

Oh, bloody good!

2   *cups milk*
1   *cup sugar*
1   *teaspoon nutmeg*
$^1/_2$ *cup light oil*
3   *eggs*
2   *packages dry yeast*
$^1/_2$ *cup warm (not too hot) water*
10 *cups sifted all-purpose flour*
1   *cup seedless currants*
    melted butter

GLAZE:
1   *cup confectioners' sugar*
2–3   *teaspoons lemon juice*

Combine milk, sugar, nutmeg and oil in a large mixing bowl.

In a separate bowl, beat eggs until frothy.

Dissolve yeast in water.

Add 2 cups flour, dissolved yeast and beaten eggs to milk mixture. Beat with rotary beater or by hand until completely smooth. Slowly add remaining flour and currants and turn onto a floured board.

Knead until smooth and elastic on a lightly floured board (approximately 10 minutes). Set in a greased bowl. Cover and allow to rise in a warm place until light and double in bulk ($1^1/_2$ to 2 hours).

Punch down and roll out in a 15-by-18-by-$^1/_2$-inch rectangle and cut with a 3-inch cookie cutter. Place buns on greased baking sheets. Brush with melted butter, cover, let rise until double in bulk (about $1^1/_2$ hours).

Using a knife or scissors, make a cross on each bun. Bake at 350 degrees for approximately 25 minutes.

Glaze each bun with icing made from the confectioners' sugar and lemon juice.

MAKES 30–35 BUNS.

SUNNY CORN BREAD

I could eat this in the desert, but you gotta have milk!

1   cup cornmeal
1   cup all-purpose flour
1/2 cup sugar
4   teaspoons baking powder
1   egg
1/2 teaspoon vanilla
1   cup milk (or 1 10-oz. can creamed corn)
1/4 cup vegetable oil

Mix dry ingredients together. Add egg, vanilla, milk or creamed corn and oil. Beat just until smooth, approximately 1 minute (don't overmix). Pour batter into a greased 8-inch square pan or greased muffin tin.

Bake at 350 degrees for approximately 20 to 25 minutes.

Serve warm with butter or covered with creamed chicken, fish or meat.

Serves 6.

Me, a young comedian, under the influence of the great one, Jackie Gleason!

OATMEAL MUFFINS

A cup of coffee, an oatmeal muffin and you.

2	*egg whites (or 1 egg)*
1/3	*cup pure maple syrup*
1	*cup skim milk*
4	*tablespoons freshly squeezed orange juice*
1	*teaspoon vanilla*
1	*teaspoon cinnamon*
1	*teaspoon allspice*
1	*teaspoon cloves*
1	*teaspoon nutmeg*
1	*tablespoon orange zest*
1 1/2	*cups rolled oats*
1	*cup flour*
1	*teaspoon baking powder*
1/2	*cup chopped pecans*
1/2	*cup raisins or dried cranberries*

Coat a 12-muffin tin with vegetable oil spray.

In large bowl, whisk egg whites until they become frothy. While whisking add maple syrup, milk and orange juice. Then add vanilla, cinnamon, allspice, cloves, nutmeg and orange zest, and whisk again. Use a wooden spoon to stir in oats, flour and baking powder. Gently mix in pecans and raisins or dried cranberries.

Spoon batter into muffin tins so each is two-thirds full. Bake at 350 degrees until solid in center, approximately 15 to 20 minutes.

MAKES 12 MUFFINS.

ZUCCHINI OR CARROT BREAD

If the oil scares you, try 1 cup of applesauce instead.

3   *cups flour*
1½   *cups sugar*
1   *teaspoon cinnamon*
1   *teaspoon baking
          powder*
1   *teaspoon baking soda*
3   *cups shredded unpeeled
          zucchini (or replace
          with 3 cups shredded
          carrots)*
1   *cup raisins*
1   *cup chopped nuts
          (walnuts or pecans)*
3   *eggs (or egg
          equivalent), beaten*
2   *teaspoons vanilla*
1   *cup oil*

Thoroughly mix flour, sugar, cinnamon, baking powder, baking soda, zucchini, raisins and nuts in a large bowl.

Mix together beaten eggs (or egg equivalent), vanilla and oil. Pour into flour mixture and stir until thoroughly mixed. Divide into two greased loaf pans.

Bake at 350 degrees for approximately 1½ hours.

MAKES 2 LOAVES.

DOM'S BRAIDED EASTER BREAD

My mother would always make this bread at Easter. It became very traditional. She would let me color the egg and I remember that because they were called Papooses. We played like we had made a "baby"—new life for Easter. They last a long time and are great toasted. They are excellent with a cold glass of milk. Oh and I love to dunk them in a cup of coffee! Lord, I can taste them now.

1¹/₂ cups warm water
1   package granulated yeast
1   teaspoon sugar
5   cups flour
3   large eggs
1   cup warm milk
1   cup sugar (or replace half with brown sugar)
1   teaspoon vanilla
4   tablespoons warm butter or oil
1   tablespoon orange zest
1   tablespoon lemon zest
³/₄   cup citron (minced dried fruit) (optional)
¹/₂   cup chopped nuts or raisins (optional)
1   egg, slightly beaten

In a large mixing bowl, put warm water, yeast and sugar. Stir gently, then let wait 10 minutes. Add flour, eggs, sugar, vanilla, butter or oil, orange and lemon zest and milk. Citron, 1/2 cup of chopped nuts or raisins are optional. Mix with a wooden spoon about 8 minutes. Add more milk if dough is very dry.

Turn mixture out on a floured surface and knead for about 8 minutes until smooth, form into a ball and place into a lightly greased bowl. Cover and let rise for 1^1/$_2$ hours.

Punch down dough and return to floured surface. Cut into six equal parts and roll into cigar shapes. Place two sets of three "cigars" onto a greased baking pan. Braid (makes two loaves) and let rise again about 1 hour.

Brush bread with lightly beaten egg and bake at 350 degrees for 1 hour until golden.

MAKES 2 LOAVES.

Note: You can add an egg to the braid and it will hard boil as bread cooks. You can even (Easter) color the egg.

My mother called these "Papooses."

Taralli

I was recently in Florida and I went to visit my sister-in-law, who was on vacation with her two sisters, Connie and Candida, and her husband, Tony, so Tony and I were surrounded by three Italian ladies, all excellent cooks. It was the middle of the day and we had espresso coffee and a lemon rind. They put out a dish of taralli—each sister had made their own version. We all had taralli and provolone and Jarlsberg cheese. We chatted about the old days while munching on these incredibly hard biscuits. And because they have pepper in them, your mouth sings a little song called "Oh, My." In fact, they keep your mouth so awake they gently keep you from taking a nap inadvertently.

Biting those taralli created a flashback in my mind to when I was younger and visited my relatives in Spinoso, Italy, not too far from Naples. We were all going to get up at 4 A.M. in order to remove the very top shoots of all the grape plants in the arbor. It seems that this encourages the growth of bigger and juicier grapes. I was looking forward to that.

Anyway, at 4:00 A.M. the breakfast consisted of espresso with a little piece of lemon rind and these very hard cookies; and at four in the morning it's very hard to wake up. I saw that everyone sipped the espresso and then bit down on these harder than hard taralli biscuits. In fact, they're so hard, I'll tell you the truth, by the second bite you were awake, and the black pepper in them kept you awake.

In the recipe that follows, I added the dried onion, the flavor of which I happen to like. I have tasted taralli with sage added to them, paprika, a little tomato paste and grated Italian cheese, which makes it taste a little like pizza. There's really no end to the variations by just putting a little curve on the recipe. And if you use your own teeth when you're biting into them, that's preferable.

TARALLI (ALSO REFERRED TO AS FRIZELLI)

This recipe can be halved.

6 cups self-rising flour
1 cup corn oil
4 teaspoons fennel seed
2 teaspoons coarsely ground pepper
3 teaspoons dried minced onion
1 teaspoon onion powder
2 cups very hot water from the tap

In a large bowl, mix flour, oil, fennel, pepper, onion and onion powder. Mix well and slowly add the hot water, mixing until all the water is used. Keep mixing until it forms a dough.

Remove to a flat surface and cut dough into small pieces. Roll out into cigar lengths and connect each end to form a circle. Place on an ungreased cookie sheet.

Bake in a 350-degree oven for 40 minutes.

These are hard when you bite into them and will keep a long time.

Very good with soup, salad and cold seafood (oysters, clams, etc.).

MAKES ABOUT 30 COOKIES.

A Garbageman's Son at the White House

My parents were Italian immigrants, and my father worked in the department of sanitation for 25 years. So, it really was with great delight that Carol and I found ourselves once again in Washington. We were asked to sit on the dais at a big Italian function with 3,000 Italians, more or less, honoring Danny DeVito. The fact that President Clinton and the First Lady were going to be two seats away made it all the more fun and exciting. At those functions a lot of grown-up people get up and say political things, and they're not always hysterical. The room was packed and throbbing in anticipation of the President's entrance. Just minutes before he was to arrive, somebody came over to me, grabbed my shoulder and said, "Dom, can you open the proceedings with a laugh?" I said, "Oh, yeah, sure."

I happen to like President Clinton very much and think that Hillary is very bright and quite an amazing woman. We've met them on several occasions and have had a lot of fun. I was especially happy when, as President Clinton entered, he shook my hand.

I was the first speaker introduced. I said that I was thrilled to be there, especially since the President and First Lady were there making it quite an auspicious occasion. I added that I hoped it was all right that I brought my Instamatic camera so I could take a picture, because I wanted to remember this moment forever. I said, "Mr. President, would you please come up here?" President Clinton very kindly

To Carol and Dom DeLuise
With best wishes,
and thanks

Bill Clinton

obliged. He had a big smile on his face as I handed him my Instamatic. I called Danny DeVito who got up and stood by me. Then the President of the United States, holding my Instamatic, proceeded to take a picture of Danny DeVito and me in front of 3,000 by then hysterical people.

President Clinton was such a good sport, he laughed harder than anyone. The photographers at the event took lots of pictures, and this whole event was pretty well documented. At the end of the dinner, when President Clinton was making his speech, he said that he had thought he was going to come here and be treated with love and respect. He never imagined that he would be reduced to becoming Dom DeLuise's photographer. There were a lot of laughs, and I realized that only a really big man could have taken it so well. Being the good sport that he is, everyone just liked him all the more.

After the dinner, we went into a private room with the President and First Lady, Danny DeVito and his wife Rhea Perlman, Fabio and a few other guests. The President and First Lady were very gracious as we all took a picture standing around the President. Then the President left the center of the group, took the photographer's camera, sent the photographer in to take his place next to the First Lady, and proceeded to take the picture. Everyone laughed and applauded.

The Clintons have been very kind to us, and we support them. I have campaigned for him. I have written to both of them, and they have both very graciously replied, with great humor I might add. My father and mother would be so proud. This makes me, an Italian immigrant garbageman's son, very happy. Very happy, indeed.

ITALIAN CHEESE CAKE

PASTRY:
3/4 cup sifted flour
2   tablespoons butter or margarine
1   tablespoon sherry

FILLING:
1   pound ricotta cheese
4   tablespoons flour
3/4 cup sugar
1   tablespoon lemon juice
2   eggs, separated (or egg equivalent)
1/2 cup cream, whipped

To make pastry, mix together flour and butter or margarine until mixture is the consistency of coarse meal. Add sherry, a little at a time, until pastry forms a stiff ball. Chill. Roll out on a lightly floured board and put in the bottom of a 9-inch pie pan.

Put ricotta cheese in a bowl. Add flour, sugar and lemon juice and mix well. Beat egg yolks gently and mix into the ricotta mixture. Fold the whipped cream into the mixture. Beat egg whites until stiff and gently fold into the ricotta mixture. Pour into the unbaked pastry shell.

Bake in a 300-degree oven for 1 hour. Turn off heat and leave pie in oven for another hour with door closed. Remove from oven and cool.

Then enjoy!

SERVE THIN SLICES. FEEDS ABOUT 20 PEOPLE.

MY FAVORITE SISTER ANNE FROM LONG ISLAND'S LEMON COOKIES

When my sister Anne from Long Island, where she lives with her terrific husband, Phil, who used to be in the Golden Gloves, comes to Los Angeles to visit us, they are always so impressed with our California fruit trees, especially our lemon trees. The first day they arrive, my sister Anne from Long Island picks some lemons and says okay, let's get started. I know just what she means.

So here's the recipe for my sister Anne from Long Island's Lemon Cookies and they are winners!

3/4   cup sugar
1 1/2   sticks margarine, softened
4   eggs
1 1/2   teaspoons vanilla
1/2   cup lemon juice
3 1/2   cups flour
3   teaspoons baking powder

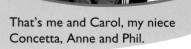

Blend the first five ingredients in a blender and pour into a bowl. Add the flour and baking powder and mix well and transfer to a flat floured surface and knead *very thoroughly.* Dough must not be sticky…may require more flour so you can work with it easily.

That's me and Carol, my niece Concetta, Anne and Phil.

Take an amount of dough about the size of an egg and roll between your hands to form a long pretzel-like stick. You may make cookies in this shape, or bring two ends together to form a small doughnut, or use a roller lightly to flatten and cut with cookie shapes or use an upside-down oiled glass.

Place cookies on a large, ungreased cookie sheet. Let stand 10 minutes at room temperature before baking. Bake at 350 degrees for 15 to 17 minutes, until lightly golden brown.

MAKES ABOUT 2 DOZEN COOKIES.

ICING (PREPARE WHILE COOKIES ARE BAKING):
1 1/4   cups confectioners' sugar
1/2   cup lemon juice

Notice how carefully Brigitte is looking at Riley and a distant relative of mine.

zest of 1 lemon (grated lemon skin)
1/2   teaspoon vanilla
        candy confetti (optional)

Put all ingredients except confetti in a mixing bowl and blend until you get the consistency of a heavy syrup. If necessary, add more lemon juice *sparingly.* When cookies are done, dip each cool cookie into the icing mixture, which will form a glaze over the cookies. Place on a dish. Sprinkle with candy confetti. Set aside until icing dries . . . and enjoy! Have some with your grandchildren and don't forget to tell 'em you love them.

I love you "Riley" with all my heart! Pass the lemon cookies. Yum!

LEMON COOKIES #2

Yes, lemons!

3   cups flour
4   eggs (or egg equivalent)
4   tablespoons light vegetable oil
1   cup sugar
1   8-oz. package nonfat cream cheese
     juice of 2 lemons
     grated rind of 2 lemons
1/2 teaspoon baking powder

GLAZE:
1 cup confectioners' sugar
   juice of 1 lemon

In a large mixing bowl, put flour, eggs, oil, sugar, cream cheese, juice of 2 lemons, grated lemon rind and baking powder. Mix well and knead into a dough.

Roll dough out to thickness of $^1/_2$ inch. Cut into circles with a cookie cutter or small upside-down glass.

Place on greased cookie sheet and bake at 350 degrees for approximately 15 minutes. Let cookies cool thoroughly.

For glaze: Mix confectioners' sugar and lemon juice in a bowl. Use enough juice to make glaze runny.

Dip top side of cookie in glaze and arrange on a serving platter.

MAKES 2–3 DOZEN COOKIES.

DOM'S APPLE PAN DOWDY

Almost no fat!

1   tablespoon butter, softened
1   cup sugar
1   egg, beaten (or egg equivalent)
1   cup flour
$^1/_2$ teaspoon cinnamon
1   teaspoon baking soda
3   cups diced, peeled apples
$^1/_2$ cup chopped nuts
1   teaspoon vanilla
1   tablespoon lemon rind
$^1/_3$ cup raisins (optional)

In a mixing bowl, cream butter, sugar and egg together.

Stir together dry ingredients and add to creamed mixture (batter will be very thick). Stir in the apples, nuts, vanilla, lemon rind and raisins (optional).

Spread into a greased 8-inch square baking pan. Bake at 350 degrees for 1 hour and 10 minutes, or until knife pulls out clean.

Serve warm or cold with whipped cream or ice cream.

SERVES 6.

DOM'S APPLE PAN DOWDY TOPPING

4   *tablespoons butter (softened)*
1/2 cup flour
1   *cup brown sugar*

Mix all ingredients until it crumbles together. Sprinkle on top of cake mixture before you put it in the oven.

Dom's little trick: If you need crumbs in a hurry, you can take slices of toasted pound cake (from the store), and break it up with your hands in a bowl. Mix with a half cup brown sugar and sprinkle it on top of your cake, before it goes into the oven. Short, sweet and delicious. Don't tell anybody you heard it from me! Mario told me! Shh!

DOM'S SISTER-IN-LAW RITA'S CHRISTMAS COOKIES

Every Christmas as sure as there's a Santa Claus, my sister-in-law Rita sends us a tin of the most unbelievably delicious cookies— *ever!* It is just amazing because the cookies maintain their goodness even though I freeze them and two months later when things have calmed down, there's Rita's cookies, which can bring back the feeling of Christmas so fast they make your tongue spin.

Here's the vital information. Thank you, Rita!

1   *cup butter*
1/4 cup sugar
1   *cup walnuts, ground*
2   *cups flour*
1   *teaspoon vanilla*
     confectioners' sugar (for coating)

In a bowl cream together butter and sugar. Add the other ingredients except confectioners' sugar. Mix well. Take 1 teaspoon of the mixture and press it into a small crescent. Place on an ungreased cookie sheet. Bake for about 10 minutes. (They do not look like they are cooked.)

Important: Let cool completely. When cooled, drop them into a bowl of confectioners' sugar. When completely coated, remove and store. They are awesome cookies!

MAKES ABOUT 50 COOKIES.

DOM'S SISTER-IN-LAW RITA'S PEANUT-BUTTER NO-COOK CHOCOLATE COOKIES

(Stand Back!)

Since this is a *no-cook* cookie, do not preheat your oven!

2 cups chopped dates
2 cups confectioners' sugar
2 cups peanut butter (smooth or chunky)

FOR DIPPING:
1 12-oz. package mini chocolate
chips, melted

In a bowl combine dates, confectioners' sugar and peanut butter and mix well. Then roll into balls about the size of a small egg yolk. Place on a tray and refrigerate.

In the meantime in a double boiler melt chocolate and dip almost all of each cookie. Set aside, cool and eat, or they freeze great!

Memorable!

MAKES ABOUT 35–40 TASTY TREATS

Ruthie and Domie

I have done a lot of work with people in show business and the one person I can be funny with anytime without thinking about it is Ruth Buzzi. We were a magic act and we were made for each other. My magician could do nothing right. He made fire appear and he would burn his hand. His assistant, Shakuntala—Ruth— was a "princess" who is in the twilight zone and is very content to stay there. We were very good together and were able to hit the comic ball back to each other and really keep it in the air.

Ruthie is hysterical and a very good cook. She once casually served these cookies and vavoom-biff-bam-boom. Then she gave me the recipe and here it is!

DOM'S FRIEND RUTH BUZZI'S
PEANUT BUTTER SURPRISE

3 cups flour
1/2 cup sugar
1/2 teaspoon baking soda
1/2 cup oil
2/3 cup peanut butter
1/4 cup light corn syrup
3 tablespoons milk
   peanut butter for center

In a bowl stir together flour, sugar and baking soda. Add the oil, peanut butter, syrup and milk and slowly work them into mixture. Shape into a long roll about 2 inches in diameter. Chill in the refrigerator for an hour.

Remove and slice 1/8 inch thick and place half the slices on an ungreased cookie sheet. Add 1/2 teaspoon of peanut butter to the center of each cookie. Cover with remaining slices. Gently seal edges with a fork. Bake in a 350-degree oven for 10 to 12 minutes. Remove from oven and let sit till cool.

They are good with milk—good alone—I mean look . . . they're just plain goooood!

MAKES ABOUT 3 DOZEN COOKIES.

DOM'S FRIEND EVE'S AMAZING CHANUKAH COOKIES

When I was a young actor I was at the Cleveland Playhouse and Caine Park Theatre in Ohio. While there I met Eve Roberts. My best friend Eve whom I have known for more years than I am allowed to mention at this time for fear this friendship which is cherished, and Carol really feels exactly the same as I do, would be famished. Anyway, Eve makes the best Chanukah cookies. Try these!

Mmmm good!

5	cups oatmeal, ground in a food processor (for a finer consistency)
4	cups flour
2	cups sugar
1	cup brown sugar
2 1/2	teaspoons baking powder
1	teaspoon baking soda
3	teaspoons vanilla
4	eggs (or egg equivalent)
1	cup melted butter or oil
2	cups mixed nuts, chopped
1	28-oz. bag chocolate chips

In a large bowl put oatmeal, flour, sugars, baking powder, baking soda, vanilla and eggs or egg equivalent. Mix well. Add the melted butter or oil, nuts and chocolate chips. Continue to mix.

Roll into small balls (about the size of a large egg yolk). Place on cookie sheets.

Bake at 350 degrees for 8 to 10 minutes. Delicious!

MAKES ABOUT 100 COOKIES.

SUGARLESS APPLE PIE

There is always this dish at our house.

3   *medium apples, peeled, cored and sliced into crescents*
$1/4$ *teaspoon cinnamon*
1   *tablespoon raisins*
1   *tablespoon nuts*
$1/2$ *cup Grape-Nuts*
1   *cup apple juice*

Place sliced apples in an 8-inch pie dish. Add cinnamon, raisins and nuts. Cover top with Grape-Nuts. Moisten with apple juice and bake at 350 degrees for $1^{1}/2$ hours.

Serve with lowfat ice cream, frozen yogurt, Häagen-Dazs or Ben & Jerry's.

SERVES 6.

BUTTER SPONGE CAKE

Patty cake, patty cake, baker man. Bake me a cake as quick as you can. Great for a birthday cake!

3   *eggs (or egg equivalent)*
1   *cup sugar*
1½   *cups sifted cake flour*
1½   *teaspoons baking powder*
½   *cup milk, scalded*
1   *teaspoon vanilla*
2   *tablespoons melted butter*

Beat eggs until they are quite light. Add sugar and beat until dissolved.

In separate bowl, sift dry ingredients together, then add to egg combination, mixing until smooth.

Allow scalded milk to cool slightly. Blend milk with vanilla and melted butter. Quickly pour milk mixture into flour mixture, stirring just until smooth and well mixed.

Generously grease two 8-by-1½-inch layer cake pans.

Pour in batter, and bake at 375 degrees for approximately 20 to 25 minutes.

SERVES 6.

MICKEY, MY FRIEND THE APPLE STRUDEL MAKER

I am an early riser and I sometimes go to the famous Farmer's Market in Los Angeles. While the birds are still singing their morning song, I have a cup of coffee. I meet other actors. We talk about show business. It's a great way to start the day. One morning I met a man who has been making apple strudel for 50 years. I was impressed. His name is Meir Jacobs. His friends call him Mickey. He really is one of the sweetest apple strudel makers I ever met. He is also the *only* apple strudel maker I ever met. His apple strudel is so good, when you're eating it everything seems absolutely perfect.

This apple strudel tastes best warm. As warm as Mickey's heart!

8–10	*sweet apples, peeled, pitted and sliced thick*
2	*tablespoons lemon juice (to prevent browning)*
1	*cup Mickey's secret ingredient: pound cake crumbs*
1	*cup seedless raisins*
1	*cup ground nuts (optional)*
1/2	*cup sugar*
1	*teaspoon cinnamon*
	filo dough flats
1	*egg, beaten*

Put all the ingredients in a large bowl, except for the filo dough flats and egg, and mix gently. Lay down two filo dough flats (sheets) and fill the center lengthwise with the mixture. Fold over the sides of the flats, and place seam-side down on a greased piece of aluminum foil on a cookie sheet. Continue until all the apple mixture is used up. Use a pastry brush to coat the top of the strudel with the beaten egg. In a preheated 375-degree oven, bake for 20 minutes. Lower heat to 325 degrees and bake for another hour.

SERVES 10–12.

Note: If you're out of pound cake, try using a cup of cookie crumbs. I once used ground chocolate chip cookies. It came out great! Don't tell my friend Mickey!

You can replace the filo dough flats if you make a really thin pastry dough.

DOM'S CHOCOLATE MOUSSE BARS

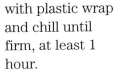

6   *extra large egg whites*
1¼   *cups sugar*
1   *tablespoon canola oil*
1½   *cups unsweetened baking chocolate, melted*
¾   *cup all-purpose flour*
⅓   *cup unsweetened cocoa powder*
1½   *cups nonfat plain yogurt*
1   *teaspoon vanilla*

Spray an 8-inch square baking pan with vegetable spray.

In a large mixing bowl whip the egg whites until frothy. Gradually add the sugar and beat until fluffy. Meanwhile, stir the oil into the melted chocolate. Add this mixture to the egg whites and blend. With a mixer on low, sift in the flour and cocoa powder and fold together. Beat until fluffy. Add the yogurt and vanilla; beat until uniformly combined.

Scrape the batter into the pan; smooth the top. Bake at 350 degrees until the batter in the center feels firm to the touch, but a toothpick comes out coated with the batter, 30 to 35 minutes.

Remove the pan to a wire rack to cool to room temperature. Cover with plastic wrap and chill until firm, at least 1 hour.

MAKES 16 BARS.

Brunch with Carol's brother George Arata, his wife Midge, and the rest of the Arata family.

BROWNIES

So small, so tasty, so—
sew your pants!

2¹/₂ *squares unsweet-*
      ened chocolate
¹/₃   *cup oil*
1   *cup sugar*
2   *eggs (or egg*
      equivalent)
¹/₂   *cup self-rising*
      cake flour
¹/₂   *cup walnuts,*
      chopped
1   *teaspoon vanilla*

Melt chocolate squares
with oil in a small
saucepan. In a mixing
bowl, combine sugar and
eggs. Blend in melted
chocolate mixture. Sift in
flour. Stir in vanilla and nuts. Using a square 8-by-8-by-2 inch greased
pan, pour dough in evenly.

   Bake at 350 degrees approximately 20 to 25 minutes, until a knife
pulls out clean.

   Allow to cool before cutting into squares.

SERVES 8.

TRIFLE

Don't trifle with me, sir!

1   *package regular vanilla pudding and pie filling mix*
2$^1/_2$ *cups milk*
1   *7-inch packaged sponge layer cake*
1   *cup sherry*
$^1/_2$ *cup raspberry jam*
8   *almond macaroons (optional)*
1   *cup heavy cream, whipped*
       glazed cherries
       slivered almonds

Begin preparing early: Make vanilla pudding as instructed on package.
Use 2$^1/_2$ cups milk for the pudding. Set wax paper directly on the surface
of the pudding. Chill in refrigerator.

   45 minutes before serving: Quarter sponge cake, then cut each quarter crosswise.

   Set out 8 dessert dishes and place one slice of cake in each dish, cut
side up. Pour sherry over evenly, and allow to soak for $^1/_2$ hour.

   Spread raspberry jam on top of each slice, then crumble macaroons
on top, if desired. Pour vanilla custard sauce evenly over each slice. Top
with whipped cream, cherries and almonds.

SERVES 8.

Christopher Santoro

In 1988 when I wrote the book *Eat This: It'll Make You Feel Better,* the publisher told me it was doing well. They asked if I wanted to venture forth into children's books. I wrote *Charlie the Caterpillar.* God bless America! It was well received by children and parents alike.

When you write a cookbook, you need recipes. When you write a children's book, you need an illustrator. In any case, Simon and Schuster in essence arranged a blind date for me with an illustrator named Christopher Santoro. I had never met the man before and a package with his take on *Charlie the Caterpillar* arrived at my home. I was thrilled, tickled and delighted. By the end of the book I was moved to tears. Who was this man? His talented pen could move me to tears and so enhance my stories that it was as if I was reading them for the first time. I wrote moments in the story and Christopher with his imagination expanded them further than my vision. I was really thrilled. Do you think we can get Christopher Santoro to collaborate with me again? My spirited editor said, "That's who we have. Chris has your galleys and is working on them as we speak," "All right!" I said, feeling blessed. Which is exactly what I was when we finished working on *King Bob's New Clothes.* Then Christopher and I had a talk and his incredible humor and insight helped me solve problems I had with *Hansel and Gretel.* It had to be fun, humorous, a little scary but not too scary. I think we accomplished that in our version of *Hansel and Gretel* which I am very proud of! Then, it was another small but significant chat I had with Chris that helped me crystallize the path I would take while writing *The Nightingale,* which came out sweet and tender and very magical. Very magical indeed. I am proud to say that we have in the works *The Adventure of the Country Mouse and the City Mouse.* I love and respect Christopher Santoro, his talent, insight and sweet nature. I thank God every day for my blind date with Christopher Santoro, my illustrator, my friend. This is a merger made in heaven. How lucky can you get? I asked him what his favorite food in the whole world was and he said, "Rice pudding." I said, "Christopher, I have a sister, Anne, that makes the best rice pudding you'll ever taste!... And here it is!

DOM'S LUSCIOUS RICE PUDDING

3   *eggs*
1   *cup sugar*
1   *tablespoon vanilla*
1   *quart milk*
2   *cups cooked rice*
1/2 *cup raisins*
     cinnamon

Mix the eggs, sugar and vanilla in a bowl and beat well. Add the milk, rice and raisins, stir gently and put in a large greased casserole dish. Lightly sprinkle the top with cinnamon. Place the dish in a larger pan with water in it (it's like you're creating a double boiler). Bake at 350 degrees for 1 hour. Remove and let sit for about 20 minutes.

I like this when it's at room temperature and no one is around to count how many portions I'm having.

YIELDS ENOUGH PUDDING FOR 15–20 SERVINGS.

Closing Thoughts

Writing *Eat This Too* has been an experience I shall always cherish. While gathering the new recipes and often new friends—something I deeply enjoyed and found lots of energy for—I discovered something that was very important to me! Since people had access to *Eat This* I found that I was often approached as if they already knew me. It was a revelation to me. If I was in a theater in New York walking along Broadway, or in New Orleans and being mistaken for Paul Prudhomme, or in a movie studio in Los Angeles, or swimming in Florida, or even on a ride in Disneyland, I realize that people are so very generous, so willing, with warm humor and with a sincere invitation, to share with you what's in their hearts. That with all the troubles we have, and we all have our share inside all of us (where the child in us lives), there is a lot of good. I thank all the people I have ever met over the years for helping me to remember that.

Every time I meet a new family and we talk a while, I realize how very similar we all are. To these people who generously shared so many of their recipes, I thank them with all my heart. And to those people who shared with me what was in their hearts, know that it made all the difference. As I get older and probably wiser,

I realize it's my wife and family that mean the world to me. I pray I can stay around long enough to keep appreciating them. I wish you the same!

I do hope you enjoy *Eat This Too!* but more than that, I wish you health, happiness, a good appetite and Love,

Dom DeLuise

Index

Photo Credits

Bert Andrews Photography, page 93

AP/Wide World Photos, page 27

© Berliner Studio, page 94

Blazing Saddles © 1974 Warner Bros. Inc., page 105

© Photo courtesy of Mrs. Brisby Ltd., page 146

Courtesy of Brooklyn Union/Ted Beck, photographer, page 78*

Cannonball Run II © 1983 Arcafin B.V. and Warner Bros. Inc., page 95

CBS Photo Archive, page 106

Dennis Chalkin, page v (top right)

Robert Clary. Paintings by Robert Clary reprinted with his permission, pages 174 (top right), 175

Bob D'Amico/ABC, page 7 (top left)

© Disney Enterprises, Inc., page 238 (bottom right)

Davis Factor/FOX, page 198

J. Peter Happel Photography, pages 77, 209

© Al Hirschfeld. Art reproduced by special arrangement with Hirschfeld's exclusive representative, The Margo Feiden Galleries Ltd., New York, pages 8 (bottom left), 9

Dan Kellachan, page 248 (top left). Taken backstage at Westbury Music Fair in Westbury, Long Island, NY

Photos courtesy of Shari Lewis, pages 121, 122

David Luttrell Photography, page 248 (bottom right)

Metropolitan Photo Service, page 237

NBC/Globe Photos, Inc., pages 132, 133

Jose A. Pereyra, photographer, The Photo Studio, Durham, North Carolina, pages ii, 58–59, 110, 128–29, 151, 204–05, 216–17, 246 (top left)

Premiere Artists Agency, page 5 (top left)

Nate Silverstein, page 33

NASA, page 114 (top right)

Official White House photos, pages 218, 219

Don Stotter Advertising, page 74

© 1970 *The Twelve Chairs,* Courtesy of Brooksfilms Limited. All rights reserved, page 46

Ed Wassell, page 6 (top right)

Anne White, Hollywood, CA, pages viii, 15, 123, 202, 226

Avery Willard, page 189

Alan Zenuk, pages 102, 119, 191

* Welcome Back to Brooklyn Festival, sponsored by Brooklyn Union, the Borough President's Office and the Fund for the Borough of Brooklyn, is an annual celebration which honors the many great luminaries from Brooklyn.

Dom cooks with and loves "Tools of the Trade" pots.

Acknowledgments

I wish to give special thanks to Sammy Johnson and Stephanie Bonë of North Carolina who were such sweet help with the cover picture. And many, many, thanks to Judith Lovejoy. I would also like to thank Meryl Levavi, Jane Cavolina and Brett Freese for their creativity and amazing patience while compiling this here book!

Eat This is now on Video!

Join Dom DeLuise, King of Comedy and Cooking, as he takes the fun one step further and invites you on a cooking spree in his kitchen and demonstrates delicious recipes for *Eat This...It'll Make You Feel Better!,* Dom's best-selling cookbook.

In *Eat This—The Video #1,* you'll experience all the charm of Dom's book as you journey with him back to Brooklyn. You'll laugh as you learn while Dom and Mom turn their wonderful Italian recipes into a family feast. Anyone who has a mother, loves to cook, eat or laugh, will want this video as their very own.

Eat This—The Video #1 includes many of his most tantalizing recipes and is only $8.88, plus $4.95 for postage and handling. California residents add 8.25% sales tax.

After you've cooked everything in *Eat This—The Video #1,* be sure to order Video #2, 3 and 4 to complete your comedy cooking course!

To order *Eat This—The Video* (by M/C or Visa) call TOLL-FREE:
1-800-794-7988

Or send check or money order to: EAT THIS—THE VIDEO
P.O. Box 1801
Pacific Palisades, CA 90272

Allow 3 weeks for delivery.

You can also visit Dom's Web site at: www.bbco-op.com.dom_deluise

About the Author

Dom DeLuise says it best himself:

Beside writing children's books and this cook-book, I've been lucky enough to have worked in seventy-six films and to have done the voices for animated features such as *The Secret of Nimh, Oliver and Company, An American Tail, Fievel Goes West, All Dogs Go to Heaven* 1 and 2. I am in the midst of a television series. I also have the pleasure of doing a nightclub act. I perform magic (badly), talk, sing, bring audience members on stage. I get a big kick out of doing nightclubs. I work at Resorts International, Golden Nugget in Atlantic City, Harrah's, Bally's and The Sahara in Las Vegas. I worked with a wonderful, talented conductor, Dan Strickland, for ten years. I am now working with Sal Sicari, who is terrific for me. Sal, his wife Geri and I have had laughs for twenty years. Nightclub work is very demanding but it tickles my heart.

When my amazing mother was alive, she came often to see my show. I am very happy when any of my, or Carol's, family come to see my work. It gives me great joy!

Geri, me and Sal. Friends forever.

Dick and Pat Van Patten, the late Jack Gilford and his wife, Madeline, and Carl and Estelle Reiner all came to visit me in Westbury, Long Island.

I was performing with Phyllis Diller, who is an hysterical lady, as we all know. But contrary to what you might think of her, Phyllis is one of the

Dick and Pat Van Patten, Jack and Madeline Gilford, Estelle and Carl Reiner, Carol and me. What joy!

classiest broads I have ever worked with.

All these people were in the audience and I was flabbergasted. Oh, it's great to have relatives and it's easy to understand why they might like you, having the same blood and all, but this group were my peers who I knew socially. Just the fact that they were in the audience is a thrill that is accompanied by a very flattering feeling that they are in fact validating you in a very sweet, warm way that touches your heart. So when I look at this picture of these people who I love and respect, I get all choked up. We all went out and had a late-night supper. I remember the veal being particularly delicious that night. Both my hunger and emotional needs were fully satisfied.

The great Phyllis Diller, me and my sweetheart, the one and only Dolly Parton.